10-04

IMAG
of America

DECATUR

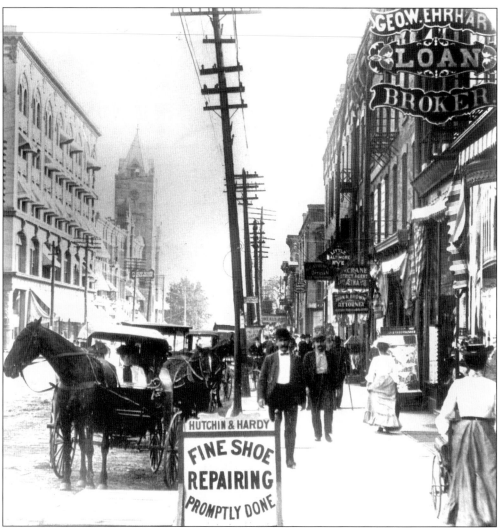

VIEW OF WATER STREET, 1904. This view of downtown Decatur taken by C.L. Wasson, Decatur's most famous photographer, shows real horses and buggies crowded on Water Street just before the "horseless carriages" began to appear. Note the brick street, shoe repair, and pawnbroker signs, and the little tavern down the block offering rye whiskey. (Courtesy Macon County Historical Society.)

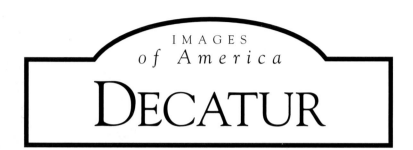

IMAGES
of America

DECATUR

Dan Guillory

ARCADIA

Published by Arcadia Publishing
Charleston SC, Chicago IL, Portsmouth NH, San Francisco CA

Printed in Great Britain

Library of Congress Catalog Card Number: 2004107380

For all general information contact Arcadia Publishing at:
Telephone 843-853-2070
Fax 843-853-0044
E-mail sales@arcadiapublishing.com
For customer service and orders:
Toll-Free 1-888-313-2665

Visit us on the internet at http://www.arcadiapublishing.com

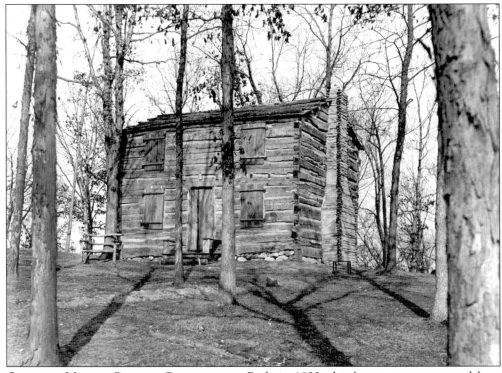

ORIGINAL MACON COUNTY COURTHOUSE. Built in 1830, this log structure was used by a young lawyer, Abraham Lincoln, in 1838. The next year, it was moved to the east side of town and a brick building was erected on the spot. This photo shows the courthouse as it looked in March 1909 at one of its locations in Fairview Park. Ultimately, the old structure was moved to the Frontier Village on the grounds of the Macon County Historical Society's North Fork Museum. It has been restored several times, and some of its present logs were taken from Warnick's Tavern after that building burned down in 1975. (Courtesy Decatur Public Library.)

CONTENTS

Acknowledgments

I must begin by kindly thanking John Hallwas and Bill Furry, who first suggested the idea of this book. And I owe a special debt to the following local historians and scholars, who patiently endured my seemingly endless questions on fine points of Illinois history and culture: Bob Sampson, Brent Wielt, Dayle Irwin, Nancy Torgerson, and Kim Bauer. Thanks also to Liz Jobe of Arcadia for her unfailing good spirits, kindness, and professionalism.

Archival images from many institutions helped to make this book possible, including the Abraham Lincoln Presidential Library, Millikin University, the Macon County Conservation District, the Macon County Historical Society, and the Local History Room of the Decatur Public Library—to which I was given full access by Lee Ann Fisher, the city librarian. Other librarians, technical staff, and volunteers who helped in large and small ways include: Sandi Pointon, Jerrald Merrick, Bev Hackney, Arthur Gross, Carol Robinette, Junie Longbons, Matt Wilkerson, David Rush, Larry Bechtel, and Doug Imboden. Special thanks to Deb Kirchner of Millikin U, and to Pat Riley for generously sharing his collection of Decatur postcards and other ephemera. And, although they were gone by the time of this book, I do hope that Charlotte Meyer and Florence White persist somewhere in the spirit of these pages.

This book is dedicated to the three ladies in my life: Lilly, Leslie, and Gayle.

–D.G.

INTRODUCTION

The scene was as still as a watercolor. Surface ice had just melted on the Sangamon River, and the green waters rose a little higher each week as spring rains poured into the creeks and ravines that bordered the meandering stream. In a few weeks, spring flowers would push up through the leafy mast of the woodland floor—phlox, bluebells, violets, and wild hyacinths. Dogwood and redbud would burst into sprays of pink, white, and magenta blossoms. Only a few cabins stood in makeshift clearings, and some years earlier the last Algonquin-speaking Kickapoos had left the area forever.

In 1829, out of this green landscape (originally part of Shelby County), the state legislature carved Macon County and designated Decatur as the county seat. The name Decatur was taken in honor of Commodore Stephen Decatur, a very popular hero of the day, although he had no obvious ties to the place. Some 50 counties and cities across the United States also chose to honor the Commodore, including Decatur, Alabama; and Decatur, Georgia.

Decatur was fortunate to count many bright lights among its first residents, including this impressive dozen: Leonard Stevens (Stevens Creek is named after this first permanent settler); John Hanks (a neighbor of Stevens, relative of the Lincoln family, and splitter of rails with young Abe Lincoln in the summer of 1830); William Warnick (first sheriff of Macon County; neighbor of the Lincolns, 1830–1831); Captain David Allen (built a sawmill on the Sangamon in 1831 and later became a major real-estate developer); Benjamin Austin (Macon County surveyor who platted the City of Decatur); Isaac C. Pugh (storekeeper and brigadier general in the Civil War); "Uncle Jimmy" Renshaw (tavern-keeper who knew Lincoln); Dr. H.C. Johns (livestock specialist who married Jane Martin); Jane Martin Johns (author of *Personal Recollections*, a detailed memoir of Decatur's early days); David S. Shellabarger (first "grain baron" of Decatur); Jasper J. Peddecord (merchant, meat-packer, and banker); and James Millikin (banker, investor, and philanthropist who founded Millikin University in 1903). This list omits important figures like Richard Oglesby, Hieronymus Mueller, A.E. Staley, and many others. Fortunately, there exists a good photographic record of Decatur's leading citizens between 1860 and 1910.

Although Decatur farmers regularly brought in abundant crops of corn, oats, and wheat, there was no economical way to ship that grain to market in St. Louis or Chicago. But that situation changed dramatically in 1854, when the Great Western Railroad arrived from the west and the Illinois Central Railroad from the north, making Decatur a true "crossroads city." Suddenly grain processors had access to nearly insatiable markets and local residents could buy the same stoves, china, magazines, and ready-made clothing available to consumers on the east coast. On May 10, 1860, Abraham Lincoln was first nominated for the presidency in a wigwam near Central Park in Decatur, and in the ensuing Civil War Macon County gave five generals to the war effort and many fighting men, like the 116th Regiment. Meanwhile, the industrial expansion continued.

In the 1870s, Decatur came of age with a powerful sense of self-consciousness and purpose. E.A. Gastman, a nationally-known educator, was already showing impressive results in his grand plan to strengthen Decatur schools (begun in 1862). In 1870, the Decatur Rolling Mill began making iron rails, and in 1871 Decatur published its first *City Directory*. Then, in rapid-fire sequence, the following milestones occurred: establishment of a streetcar system in 1876, founding of the YMCA and St. Mary's Hospital in 1877–1878, and the publication of the *Decatur Review* in 1878 and the *Decatur Herald* in 1880, which served the city for a century until they were combined in 1981 to form the present *Herald Review*.

By the turn of the century, Decatur was proudly celebrating its status as a center for grain processing, general manufacturing, and banking. Decatur's Richard Oglesby had served as governor three times (more than any other citizen), James Millikin had begun plans for Millikin University, and Hieronymus Mueller had invented a self-tapping valve for city water mains that is still sold all over the world. A.E. Staley would bring his "Cream Corn Starch" brand to Decatur in 1909 before pioneering the processing of the unfamiliar soy bean in 1922, helping Decatur to earn its sobriquet of "Soy City." And it is said that nearly every submarine launched by the U.S. Navy in World Wars I and II contained pumps, valves, and fittings manufactured in Decatur.

In the 1980s and 1990s, Decatur suffered the same ailments that afflicted all the "rustbelt" cities—unemployment, high inflation, outsourcing, downsizing, and other effects of the new global economy. Mueller, General Electric, Borg-Warner, and Firestone were either bought out or closed down, and A.E. Staley became Tate and Lyle. Caterpillar and Archer Daniels Midland ("Supermarket to the World") flourished, however. Decatur celebrated its 175th anniversary in 2004, at a time when substantial downtown renovation (Demirco Place) and a new housing development (Wabash Crossing) were underway. To some extent, Decatur has always been at a crossroads, but even a brief review of its history shows ample reservoirs of creativity and the makings for a rich and rewarding future.

One

THE LINCOLN ERA
1829–1869

On March 14, 1830, Thomas Lincoln and his family arrived in the rustic village of Decatur, traveling in a caravan of three wagons (one driven by his son Abraham) all the way from Spencer County in southern Indiana. They settled on the north bank of the Sangamon, a few miles outside Decatur, and survived the Winter of the Great Snow (1830–1831). Snow and ice accumulated to a depth of several feet on the prairie, and all living things suffered miserably. In the spring of 1831, Thomas and Sarah Bush Lincoln moved to Goose Nest Prairie near Lerna, Illinois, while Abraham went west to the hamlet of New Salem, north of Springfield.

Abraham Lincoln next appeared on the record of Decatur in 1838, when he helped try a case in the old log courthouse. Lincoln, as a lawyer with the eight circuit, often passed through Decatur, staying at the Revere House and buying his bread from a local baker before returning to his home in Springfield. He was in Decatur in 1849, helping Jane Johns move her piano, and he participated in a crucial meeting of newspaper editors in Decatur in February 1856, a meeting that helped to define the policies of the emerging Republican Party. And on May 10, 1860, he was first nominated for the presidency in a hastily-built wigwam at the edge of Central Park. It was there that Richard Oglesby led the cheers and coined the slogan "Lincoln the Rail Candidate." Oglesby had used Decatur as something of a home base between service in the Mexican War and the California Gold Rush—the source for the names of Cerro Gordo and Eldorado Streets. Lincoln last appeared in Decatur on February 11, 1861, and Oglesby went off to war, serving under General Grant in Tennessee and ultimately attaining the rank of brigadier general. He was the last person to touch the living Lincoln, who died at 7:22 a.m. on April 15, 1865. Between his first and third terms as governor of Illinois, Oglesby oversaw the building of the Lincoln Memorial in Springfield, which was dedicated on October 15, 1874.

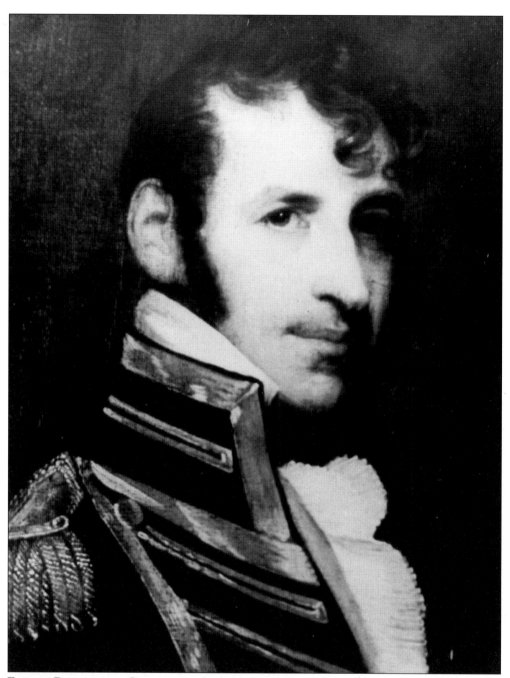

FORMAL PORTRAIT OF COMMODORE STEPHEN DECATUR. Born in 1799, he was killed in a duel in 1820, nine years before the City of Decatur was founded. He saw action in Tripoli and in the Mediterranean. Commodore Decatur also served against the British in the War of 1812. He was an extremely popular hero of the day, and a line from one of his toasts has become quite famous: "Our country right or wrong." (Courtesy Decatur Public Library.)

CALLING CARD OF A YOUNG GIRL. Between the Civil War and the turn of the century, calling cards, or *cartes de visites*, became very popular. Essentially, these images were the size of playing cards and featured a portrait of the "caller," which would be presented to the hostess on arrival or given as a keepsake. This unidentified young lady in a chair was photographed about 1860 by E.A. Barnwell of Decatur, a self-styled "Daguerrean artist and ambrotypist," who also photographed Lincoln on May 9, 1860. (Courtesy Macon County Conservation District.)

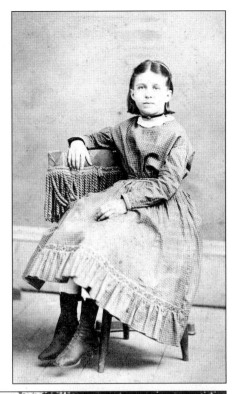

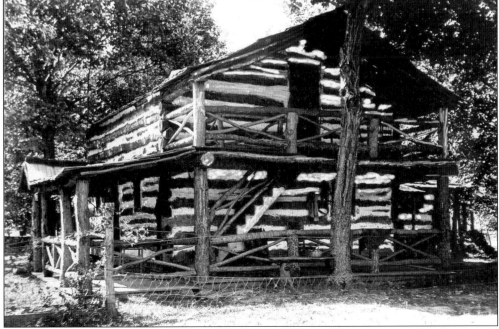

ELI ULERY'S LOG CABIN. Eli Ulery built this log cabin on the outskirts of Decatur, but his principal residence was in the town proper. He was a businessman involved in real estate. Although his cabin shows signs of renovation, it is fairly similar in size and design to the dwellings of early settlers. Photo taken about 1900. (Courtesy Decatur Public Library.)

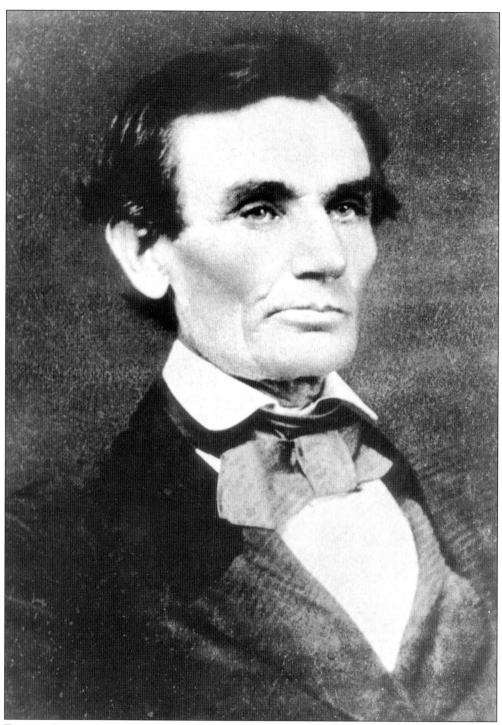

FORMAL PORTRAIT OF ABRAHAM LINCOLN. This handsome likeness of Lincoln was taken on April 25, 1858, shortly before he embarked on the famous series of debates with Senator Stephen A. Douglas. It was taken by Samuel Alschuler in Urbana, Illinois. (Courtesy Abraham Lincoln Presidential Library.)

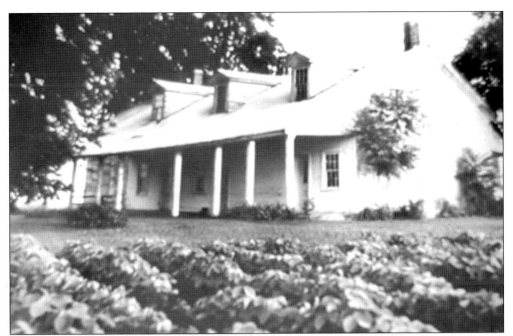

THE WARNICK TAVERN. Built in 1833, this tavern was owned by Macon County's first sheriff, William Warnick, whose home was across the road. Mrs. Warnick is said to have treated Abe's feet for frostbite in their home in March of 1831, and later Lawyer Lincoln stopped at the tavern (and stagecoach inn) on his way from Decatur to Springfield. The tavern burned to the ground in 1975, but some of its logs were saved and used in restoring the old log courthouse. (Courtesy Macon County Conservation District.)

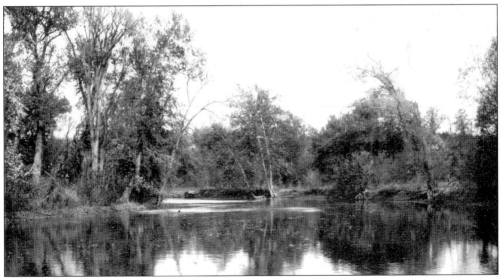

THE SANGAMON RIVER. Taken in 1896, this photo suggests the wooded and marshy quality of the banks of the Sangamon, which was so choked with debris and driftwood in the 1830s that early settlers formed committees to help clean it up. Lincoln made a speech urging the improvement of the Sangamon in Decatur in the summer of 1830, but the stream proved too shallow for commercial applications. (Courtesy Decatur Public Library.)

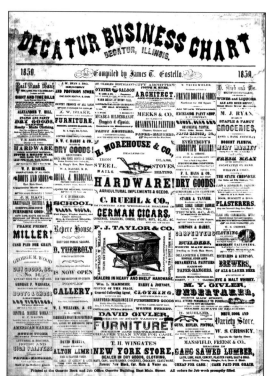

DECATUR BUSINESS CHART. Published in 1859, this general business advertisement for Decatur offers a fair idea of the variety of its merchandise and services, including stoves, cigars, plows, lumber, and shoes. The railroads had been serving Decatur for about five years when this document was originally produced. (Courtesy Decatur Public Library.)

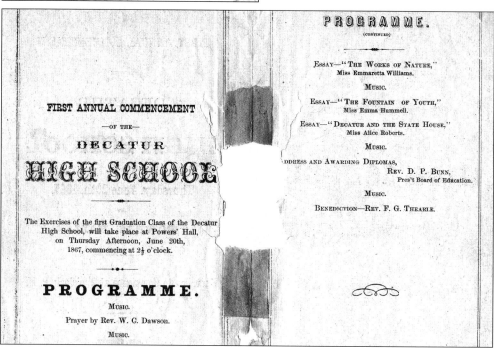

1867 COMMENCEMENT PROGRAM. The very first graduates of Decatur High School had been supervised by E.A. Gastman and attended classes during some of the bloodiest years of the Civil War. Note that the "programme" began at "2½ o'clock" and included five musical offerings, four essays, and a benediction. (Courtesy Decatur Public Library.)

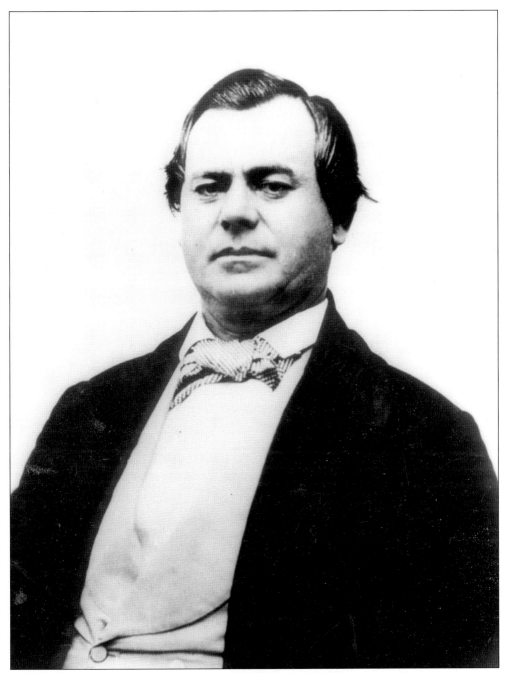

FORMAL PORTRAIT OF RICHARD J. OGLESBY. Besides being Illinois' only three-term governor and a close friend and supporter of Abraham Lincoln, Richard Oglesby was filled with a restless energy that took him from his native Kentucky to Decatur, then to Mexico, California, Europe, Tennessee, and Washington D.C. He settled finally in Elkhart, Illinois in the family home he called "Oglehurst." (Courtesy Abraham Lincoln Presidential Library.)

15

(no date)

Decatur,
Illinois.....

Decatur, ILLIN
Illinois.....
DECATUR, ILLIN
PUBLIC LIBRA

JUN 1 3 1987

LOCAL HISTOI

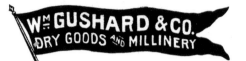

WM GUSHARD & CO.
DRY GOODS AND MILLINERY

The Greatest

Dry Goods and Millinery···· Bargain House

In Central Illinois.

There is nothing in the word

Bargain....

Unless the Price is backed up with

Quality and Style.

We don't simply try to see HOW LOW WE CAN GET THE PRICE. Our pride is to keep a good, first class article of everything we handle and give you every advantage of our Cash Purchases.

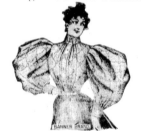

Shirt Waists.

Ladies' Shirt Waists in Percale and Madras Cloths, at 49, 69, 75, 85 and 98c. Handsomest patterns shown by any house in the city.

Dress Goods.

Thirty-six inch Silk Taffetas, Rustle Lining, all colors, and black, at 8 and 15 cents a yard.

Thirty-six-inch Black Mohair Antique 50 cents a yard.

Thirty-eight inch Black Mohair, at 65c a yard, our price, 39c.

Plain black Brilliantine, worth 50c, for 37 cents a yard.

Thirty-eight-inch Plain Black Brilliantine, worth 63c, for 47c a yard.

One case Fancy Berlin Sateens, at 12½c a yard; worth 17c.

One case Madras Cares Cloth at 17c a yard; worth 25c.

Domestics.

Two cases Shirting Prints at 3½c a yard; cheap at 5c.

Sixty-two-inch Fibre Chamois Lining, white and dark gray, 15c a yard.

Seventy-seven-inch half bleached Table Damask, at 69c.

Sixty five-inch bleached Table Damask, at 49c yard.

Three bales Good Heavy Brown Muslin at 5c a yard.

One case Yard Wide Bleached Muslin, at 4½c a yard.

One case 36-inch Percale, in all the beautiful new colorings, light, dark and medium effects, at 10c a yard. You can't match them under 15c a yard.

Bed Spreads, all ready hemmed for use, from 69c to $3.50.

A regular 10c heavy Shirting, full width, 8½c a yard.

Lace Curtains.

Lace Curtains, per pair, at 49, 59, 65, 75, and 98c, $1.25, 1.48, 1.98, 2.35, 2.98 up to 7.50.

Twenty-five per cent under any house in the state.

Tinsel Japanese Draperies, at 15c a yard.

Spring Underwear.

Ladies' Summer Gauze Vests at 5, 10, 12½, 15, 19, and 25c.

Ladies' Jersey Ribbed Union Suits for Spring, at 37 and 50c.

Men's Balbriggan Shirts and Drawers, 25c each; worth 50c.

Neckwear.

Very pretty line of Gent's Neckwear, from 15 to 50c. Everything new and tasty.

Nice line Ladies' Neck Wear in all the new and popular things for spring and summer wear.

Gents' Windsor ties, 5, 10, 15, and 25c.

Gents' 4 in-hand Ties, made of Wash Madras, 10c each.

Gents' 4-in-hand All Silk Ties, 25c each.

Hosiery.

One case Misses' hose, full seamless, ribbed, sizes 6 to 8½, at 10c a pair. Midnight Fast Black.

Infant's Fast Black Hose, from 5 to 25c a pair.

Misses' Fast Black Double Knee Hose, sizes 6 to 8½, at 25c a pair.

Two cases Ladies' Black or Tan Full Seamless Clipper Hose, at 10c a pair.

Parasols.

Parasols in endless variety, from 57c to $2.50. Every one a trade winner.

Full size Children's parasols from 15c to $2 each.

Edgings.

Hamburg Edging Embroidery, white and all colors, from 2c a yard up.

All Colors Torchon Laces, at 4c a yard.

Hamburg Edging and Insertion, with lace edge, from 15c a yard up to 50c.

Very pretty line in all the new shades.

Point Venice, Mattic Galoon Goods, Point Irepe and Spanish Laces, from 2c a yard to 75c.

Valenciennes Lace in Cream or white, 2½ inches wide, at 7½c a yard.

Notions.

Ladies' Black Sew Mitts, 15, 19, and 25c a pair.

Kid Gloves, at 75c, worth $1.

Kid Gloves, at $1, worth $1.50. Warranted.

One hundred dozen Turkish Bath and Castile Soap, at 4c a cake, or three cakes for 10c.

Pears' Soap, 10c a cake.

Pencil Tablets, 1c each.

Box Stationery, 24 envelopes and 24 sheets of writing paper, at 5, 10, 15 and 25c a box.

Tinsel Soutach Braid, 31c a bolt; worth 75c.

Rubber tipped Lead Pencils, 1c each.

Silk O-nyed Frilled Elastic, at 10c yard.

Seventy-five dozen six-hook Clasp Summer Corset, one piece steel, worth 50c, at $1.

Complete line of Fancy Hair Pins and Ornaments.

Complete line of Side Comb, at 5, 10, 15, 20 and 35 cents.

Gushard's Special Corsets,

in Black, Drab or White, at 50c. Best on earth for the money.

Bust Supporters and Bicycle Waists, $1 each.

Boy's Waists, from 19 to 75c.

Wrappers.

Banner Brand Ladies' Wrapper, made of good, strong Calico, Percales and Novelty Mixture, at 69c, 79c, 98c, $1.25, $1.75—light or dark shades, all pretty patterns and correctly made.

A complete line of Gilt Steel and Pearl Buttons, from 5c to $1 a dozen.

Waist Sets—4 buttons and cuff buttons—the set for 15 and 25c, in Pearl, Gold or Aluminum.

Dandy knitting Silks, 10c a spool.

Ladies' Garters, Gilt and Silver Buckles, 18c a pair; cheap at 25c.

Ladies' Back Combs, 5, 10, 15 and 20c.

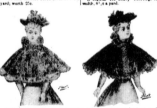

78 Capes, manufacturers' samples in silk, velvet, and cloth, at 50 cents on the dollar of actual value. Prices range from $1.98 to $4.98, worth double.

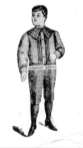

WILLIAM GUSHARD & COMPANY. William Gushard & Company, Linn and Scruggs, and "Cheap Charley" (Bachrach) were among the most successful Decatur clothiers. This advertisement was published in 1862 and republished in 1896, showing the American love of nostalgia and a general fascination with the past, especially old advertisements. (Courtesy Decatur Public Library.)

GAR ENCAMPMENT SOUVENIR. The Grand Army of the Republic, easily the most famous veterans organization in our nation's history, was formed in Decatur in 1866. This souvenir card was issued by the Wabash RR to commemorate a St. Louis event in 1887. Several famous GAR encampments also occurred in Gettysburg, Pennsylvania. (Courtesy Patrick Riley.)

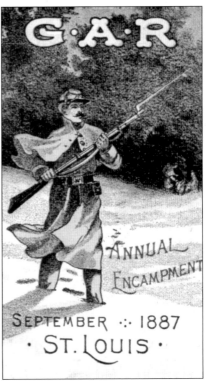

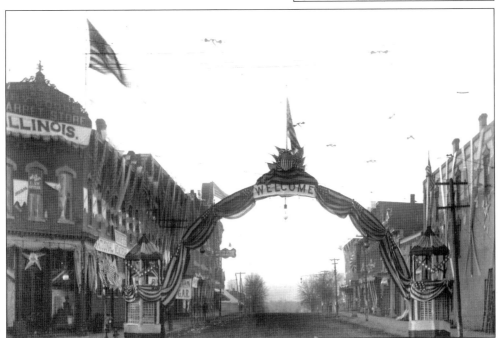

GAR ENCAMPMENT IN DECATUR. This photograph has been identified as one of the few images of the 1926 GAR meeting in Decatur. Note the electric streetcar cables overhead. The GAR became the model for the American Legion and the Veterans of Foreign Wars. By the 1930s, most of the GAR membership was deceased. (Courtesy Macon County Historical Society.)

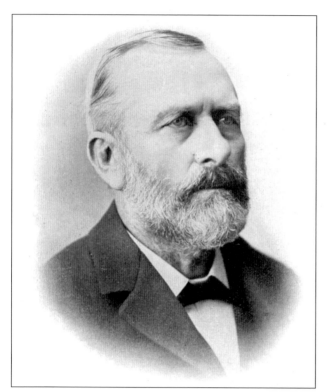

PORTRAIT OF JAMES MILLIKIN. Millikin came to Decatur in 1856, and at the time of his death in 1909, he was one of the richest men in downstate Illinois. His fortune was built initially on sheep and cattle, which he drove to Illinois from his native Pennsylvania. His homestead (1876) is on the National Register of Historic Places, and Millikin University (1903) now enrolls over 2,000 students. (Courtesy Millikin University.)

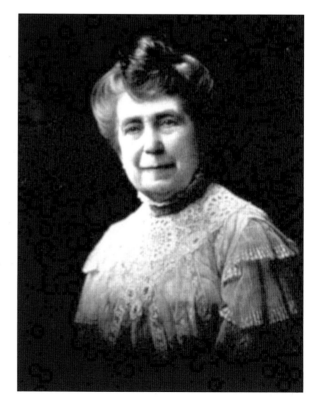

PORTRAIT OF ANNA MILLIKIN. Anna Millikin, daughter of a local Presbyterian minister, married James in 1857. She was active in the Decatur Art Club for many years and also founded the Anna Millikin Home for dependent girls and elderly women (now the site of Oakland Hall). There is a legend that a special pathway was cut through the woods between the Millikin Homestead and Aston Hall, the new women's dormitory, so that Anna could perform nightly bed-checks on the young scholars. (Courtesy Millikin University.)

Two
CITY OF INVENTIONS
1870–1929

At one time or another, Decatur has been a manufacturing and grain-processing center that produced whiskey, corn meal, beer, corn syrup, woolen underwear, wagons, carriages, coffins, corn starch, soy meal, soybean oil, iron rails, chairs, coal (from two now-defunct coal mines), phonographs, television cabinets, road graders, trucks, engines, tires, pumps, valves, hoses, kites, plate glass, potato chips, gloves, automobiles, and dresses. The city possessed a unique concentration of skilled labor and a rich inventory of spare parts and materials. Most importantly, Decatur had a culture of creativity that fostered invention and tinkering on many levels. As John Knoepfle said in his poem, "Decatur," "they make everything in this steam crowned city."

Local inventions include the Walrus soda fountain machine, the Gatling gun, the Beal corn sheller, the Graham corn planter, the Baird corn husker, the Burks pump, the Mueller water valve, and the Haworth hog ring. Less dramatic creations are breakfast corn flakes, the paint-by-number kits, roller skates, artificial (textured vegetable protein) bacon, paint-striping machines, the automobile turn-signal indicator, the flyswatter, the flexible spout ("gooseneck") oilcan, and the Bixby-Pitner "burial slippers"—bottomless shoes for the deceased.

But the inventions were not limited to the physical realm. Many visionaries and dreamers existed side-by-side with accountants and factory laborers. Orlando Powers twice built an opera house for Decatur, the Goodman Band holds the distinction of the oldest municipal band still in existence, and James Millikin dreamed of a university where the practical and the theoretical could be merged into one course of instruction. His "hybrid" vision was quintessentially part of the Decatur mindset, a mentality that joined organic and industrial wealth to produce new urban prosperity.

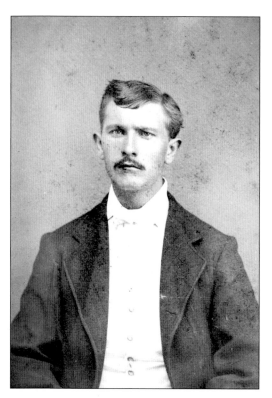

DEBONAIR GENTLEMAN, 1870S. This unidentified gentleman was photographed in the 1870s by Decatur photographer R.H. Piper, one of a number of distinguished craftsmen working in the city, although some remained only a few months. Newspapers did not hire regular staff photographers until the 1930s, so the portrait-takers supplemented their income with freelance shots of fires, parades, and public meetings. (Courtesy Macon County Conservation District.)

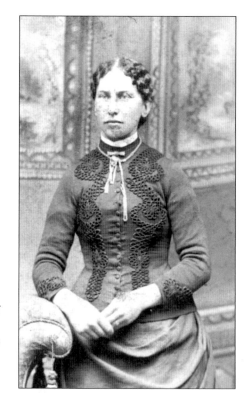

CURLY-HAIRED WOMAN, 1880S. This lady was photographed by J. Haws of Decatur. Her dour expression and relatively stiff posture—in spite of the attempt at "informality" with the hands— were dictated by the slow-acting photo-chemicals and relatively poor lenses of the day. Even slight movements produced blurred effects. (Courtesy Macon County Conservation District.)

DECATUR HIGH SCHOOL REUNION, 1882.
This program would have marked the twentieth anniversary of E.A. Gastman's tenure as principal of the Decatur School System. He planned to make the Decatur schools second to none, and in large measure he succeeded. This high school reunion was held at Smith's Opera House, the first such establishment in Decatur. (Courtesy Decatur Public Library.)

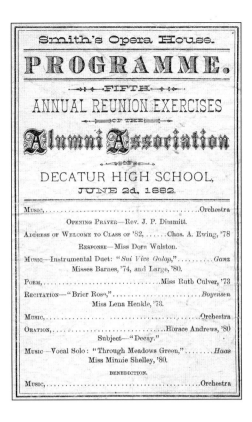

Smith's Opera House.

PROGRAMME.

FIFTH

ANNUAL REUNION EXERCISES

OF THE

Alumni Association

OF THE

DECATUR HIGH SCHOOL,
JUNE 2d, 1882.

MUSIC, ... Orchestra
    OPENING PRAYER—Rev. J. P. Dimmitt.
ADDRESS OF WELCOME TO CLASS OF '82 . . . . . . Chas. A. Ewing, '78
    RESPONSE—Miss Dora Walston.
MUSIC—Instrumental Duet: *"Sui Vive Galop,"* . . . . *Ganz*
    Misses Barnes, '74, and Large, '80.
POEM, ... Miss Ruth Culver, '73
RECITATION—"Brier Rose," . . . . *Boyensen*
    Miss Lena Henkle, '73.
MUSIC, ... Orchestra
ORATION, ... Horace Andrews, '80
    Subject—"Decay."
MUSIC—Vocal Solo: "Through Meadows Green," . . . . *Haas*
    Miss Minnie Shelley, '80.
    BENEDICTION.
MUSIC, ... Orchestra

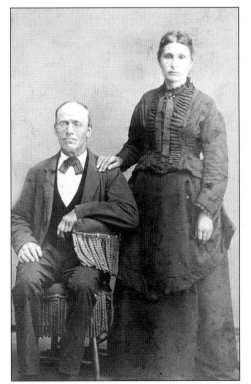

HUSBAND AND WIFE, 1870S. In what became a traditional husband-wife pose, the husband sits formally, and the wife stands at his side with her hand placed upon his shoulder. This *carte de visite* was made in the 1870s, but neither the couple nor the photographer has been identified. (Courtesy Macon County Conservation District.)

H. W. Hill Ho.

H. W. HILL,
C. P. HOUSUM.

Perry & Robinson
Syracuse N.Y

Agricultural Hardware Specialties.

Decatur, Ill., Dec 19 1881

Gentlemen: Your favor of 17th inst recd. We have no such a Ring on hand but could make one for the party. It would require some considerable change in our machinery to make a ring that large. What size wire would the party want used? What kind of wire?

What quantity will they order at one time?

The Ring would have to be forged out and made by hand that is finished up — which would be cheaper than to make patterns and have malleable castings made —

If the party will make a ring "by hand" and send in to us — we can tell better just what they want.

We judge they want the rings made open and then close them ⬭ as they used them.

We could furnish the rings either way — and adapt our machinery to complete them — Awaiting your reply we remain —

Yours Truly

H. W. Hill & Co

H.W. Hill Business Letter. This very revealing business document from the H.W. Hill Hog Ring Co. shows that the company was willing to "go the extra mile" to please a customer. Hill would tailor the products to meet the customer's precise needs at the lowest possible cost—good practices for today's entrepreneurs to emulate. The letter is dated December 19, 1881. (Courtesy Decatur Public Library.)

THREE YOUNG GIRLS, 1870S. Three young Decatur lasses strike their best poses for photographer A. Milton Lapham. They are probably in their best attire with plentiful petticoats and crinolines under their layered skirts. (Courtesy Macon County Conservation District.)

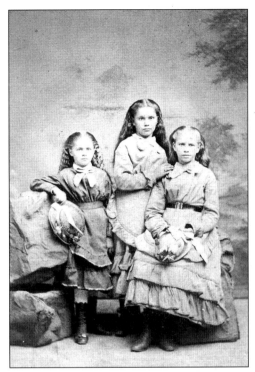

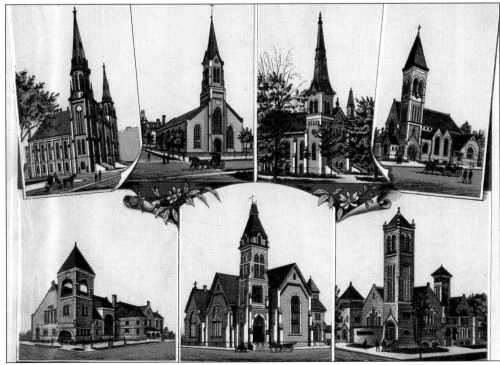

DECATUR CHURCHES, c. 1880. This scene, taken from a commemorative booklet published in Decatur about 1880, shows six Protestant houses and one Catholic house of worship. There are no mosques or synagogues at this point in most Midwestern towns. (Courtesy Patrick Riley.)

INVOICE.

H. W. Rittle
Lettick
Ills.

TRADE MARK

H. W. HILL & CO.,
AGRICULTURAL
HARDWARE*SPECIALTIES.

Decatur, Ill., Mch. 18 188 4

We ship you this day per Mail

...... Hill's Imp. Hog Ringers,		...... Adjustable Animal Markers,	
1 " Old Style "		60 ...... Animal Markers,	
...... " Hog Tongs or Holders,		...... Each Combination Tags and Rings,	
...... Cattle Tongs,		.... " Blank Tags and Rings,	
...... Hill's Pig Rings, No......		...... Letters ...... Steel Stamp at......	
...... " Shoat " No		...... Set........... Steel Alphabet,	
100 " Hog " No 3		40 ...... " .... " Figures,	
...... Bull Rings,		...... Adjustable Ladles,	
...... Calf Weaners, No. 1,		...... Housum's Barb Drivers,	
...... Cow " No 2,		...... Cases Housum's Barb for B. fences......	
Total Am't. $1 00		Received Payment,	

286885093

H. W. HILL & CO.

H.W. Hill Invoice, 1884. In 1884, as this invoice shows, a customer could buy a lot for a dollar—in this case, a hog ringer and 100 hog rings. And there was no tax to pay! It is clear that Hill was equally attentive to large and small customers. (Courtesy Decatur Public Library)

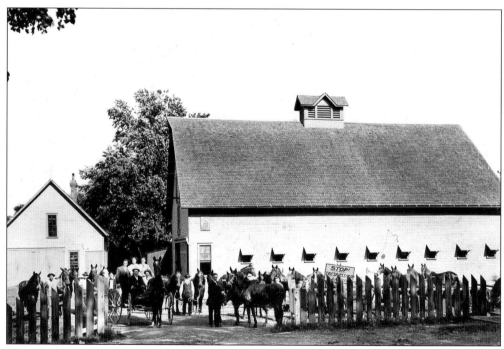

"Doc" Maffit's Ice Barn. The entire staff, horses included, turned out for this photo, taken in 1888. David A. Maffitt was a dealer in "natural and artificial ice." Natural ice was harvested from the Sangamon during the winter months, then stored in ice barns, with sawdust serving as insulation between blocks. Maffitt's barn was near the Sangamon, but his "town" residence was at 200 North Broadway. (Courtesy Decatur Public Library.)

BOY WITH STRAW HAT. This buxom boy was photographed in the late 1870s by R.H. Piper. It was customary to dress little boys and girls in similar outfits until about the age five, so the beribboned hat and fancy collar might well have been a hand-me-down from an older sister. (Courtesy Macon County Conservation District.)

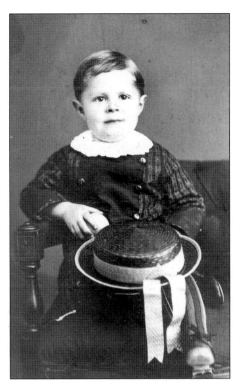

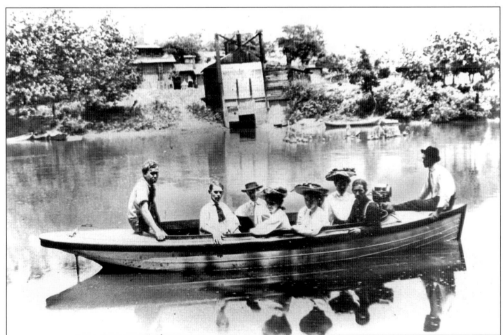

BOATING ON THE SANGAMON. This shot is a rare outdoor photograph from the period, showing a mixed party of men and women (note the gentlemen's cravats and the ladies' frilly hats) taken on a sunny day in 1890. There are virtually no photographs of pleasure-boating on the river before this time. (Courtesy Macon County Historical Society.)

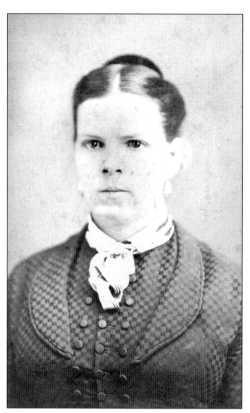

PORTRAIT OF A WOMAN, 1880s. This unidentified woman clearly loves her jewelry, as shown by the earrings and small pin on her neckerchief. Note her richly patterned and textured dress—she is clearly no pioneer woman doing farm chores on a regular basis, but a relatively well-to-do matron.

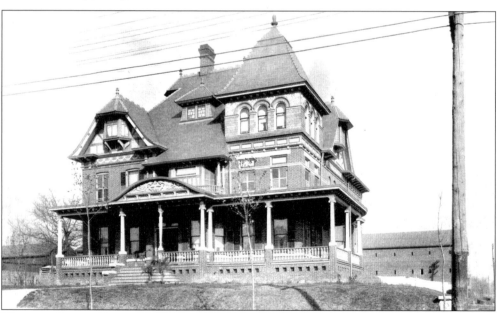

WILLIAM SHADE RESIDENCE. Turn-of-the-century Decatur abounded in Victorian Gothic houses, especially ones with turrets. This rather conservative example is the residence of William P. Shade, business partner of W.D. Brenneman, engaged in the liquor and horse cart trades, with considerable success in both. (Courtesy Decatur Public Library.)

TWO GIRLS READING. In this turn-of-the century *carte de visite* two sisters are posed together while looking at a large-format (children's?) book. Photograph by Shively Studios of Decatur. Note the lace collars on both girls and the distinctive plaid outfit on the smaller child. (Courtesy Macon County Conservation District.)

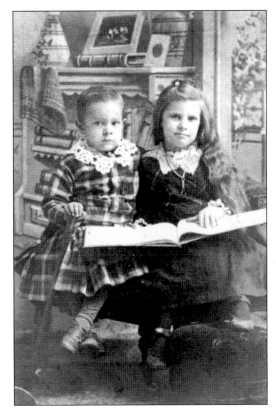

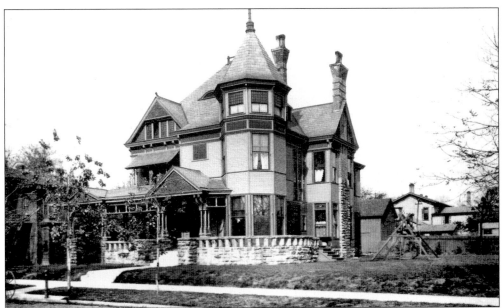

RESIDENCE OF FRANK M. YOUNG. President of the company bearing his name, businessman Frank M. Young sold "Produce & Fruits, etc." and built this turret-cornered Victorian home at 348 West Prairie. Frank is just one of many Youngs listed in the 1901 *City Directory*. (Courtesy Decatur Public Library.)

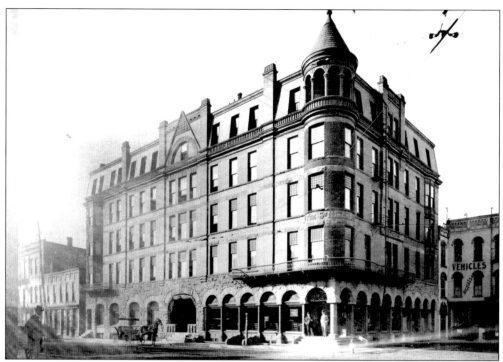

ST. NICHOLAS HOTEL. Along with the Revere House, and the Orlando, the Saint Nick was one of the most celebrated hotels in Decatur. Famous for its dining room and luxury appointments, it stood for many years on the southwest corner of Lincoln Square. This photo, taken in 1896, shows its last incarnation (minus a 10-story addition on the south side), and it survived until 1964. The GAR was created in this building. (Courtesy Decatur Public Library.)

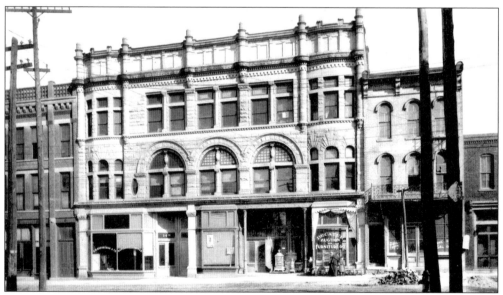

BRENNEMAN BUILDING. Taken in 1896, this photo shows the façade of the D.W. Brenneman Building at 240 North Franklin. Brenneman, who lived at 148 North Franklin, was a very successful dealer in wholesale liquor products. (Courtesy Decatur Public Library.)

FIRST PRESBYTERIAN CHURCH.
One of the landmarks of Decatur, the First Presbyterian Church building is a lovely and enduring example of Romanesque architecture. It joins with the nearby Methodist house of worship in giving Church Street its name. (Courtesy Decatur Public Library.)

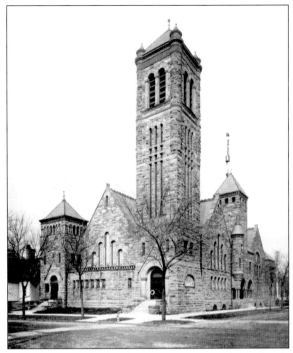

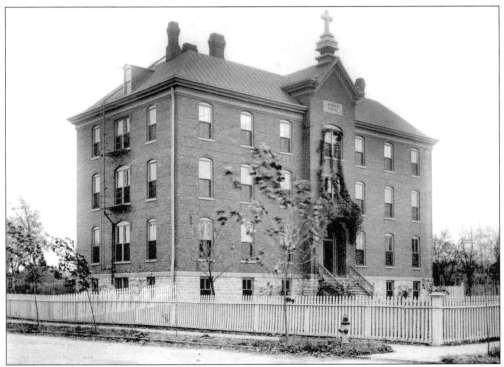

SAINT MARY'S HOSPITAL. A mainstay of Decatur's medical establishment, St. Mary's Hospital is shown in a 1896 photo taken at its original site, West Wood and Webster Streets. It has been on Lakeshore Drive since 1961, and has been undergoing another expansion since 2003. (Courtesy Decatur Public Library.)

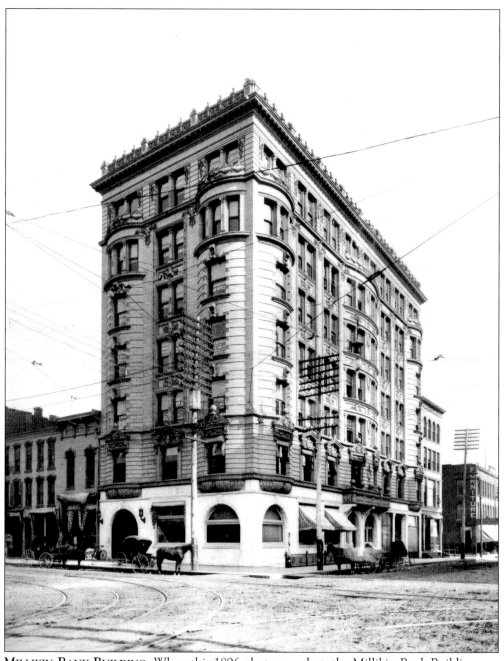

MILLIKIN BANK BUILDING. When this 1896 photo was shot, the Millikin Bank Building was brand new, but it was finally demolished in 1978, a tragic decade for historic preservation in the area. The Carnegie Library fell to the wrecking ball in 1972 and the Warnick Tavern burned down in 1975—all of which helped to raise the historical consciousness of the Decatur citizenry. The Millikin Bank Building was so important that University of Illinois architecture students regularly came to study it. Now it is a parking lot. (Courtesy Decatur Public Library.)

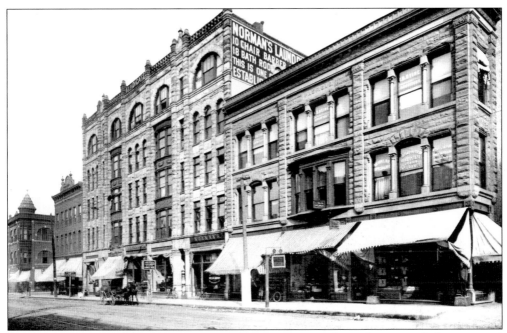

SYNDICATE AND PASFIELD BUILDINGS. These structures housed many of the principal businesses in downtown Decatur. Note the advertisement for Norman's Laundry, Barbershop, and Bath House. Norman's operated in a different form until nearly 2000. This photo dates to 1896. (Courtesy Decatur Public Library.)

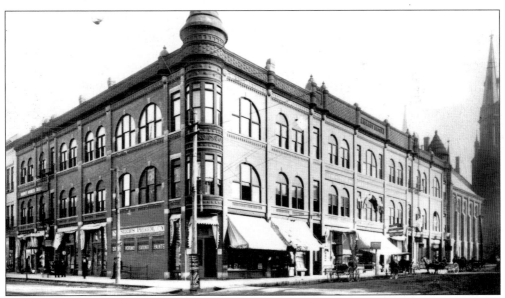

LIBRARY BLOCK. This building on the corner of Main and William Streets is another downtown landmark, virtually unchanged for over a century, now housing Haines & Essick. Under the turret is Neisler's Pharmacy (owned by W.M. Neisler) which sold, "Drinks, Perfumes, Stationery, Paints." Customers bought linseed oil and dry pigments, then mixed their own paint. The ice cream store on William Street (to the right) seems to be doing a brisk business on this warm day in 1896. (Courtesy Decatur Public Library.)

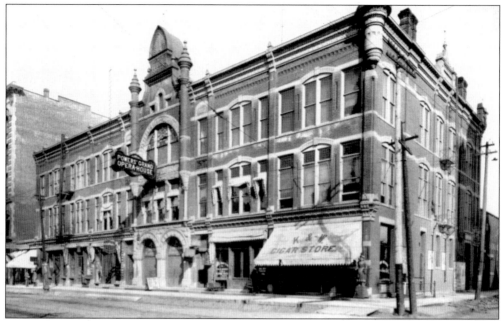

THE POWERS GRAND OPERA HOUSE. This 1896 photograph shows the "grand" opera house that was built by the scion of one of Decatur's leading families—Orlando Powers. His first opera house burned down, and fatefully so did this one. But like a proverbial phoenix rising from its ashes, the Hotel Orlando arose on the very spot, and that building still stands today. (Courtesy Decatur Public Library.)

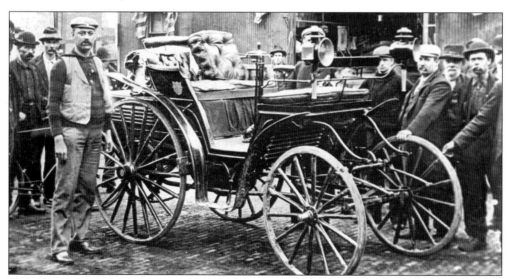

1895 BENZ AUTOMOBILE. This vehicle, imported from Germany by Hieronymus Mueller, was actually the first automobile in Central Illinois. Mueller made a number of important changes to the cooling system and other components of the car, and he was apparently poised to enter automobile manufacturing at the time of his unexpected death in 1900. Workers stand proudly around the vehicle in this 1896 photograph. Decatur did briefly enter the automobile market, with the production of the Pan American and the Comet during the World War I era. But both ventures failed. (Courtesy Macon County Historical Society.)

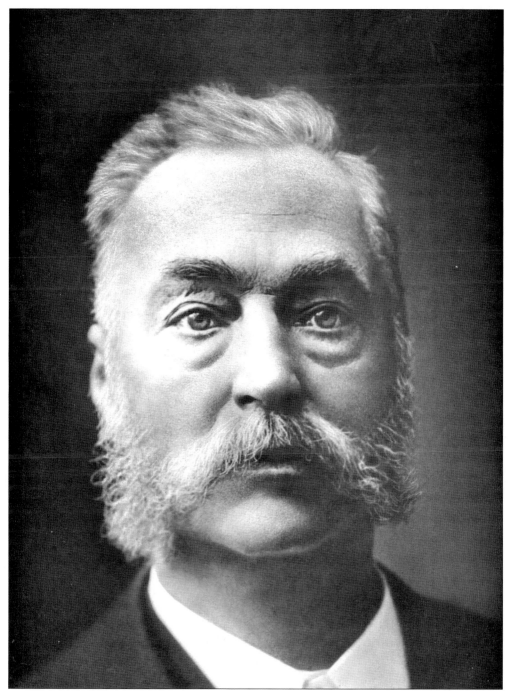

PORTRAIT OF HIERONYMUS MUELLER. Mueller, a German immigrant, came to Decatur as a gunsmith and general mechanic in 1857, and about two decades later he invented his world-famous water valve, thus becoming the grandfather of all future Decatur industrialists. He epitomizes the culture of invention and creativity. He loved to design new things, and he thrived on anything mechanical. This portrait was taken about five years before Mueller's tragic death on March 1, 1900. (Courtesy Decatur Public Library.)

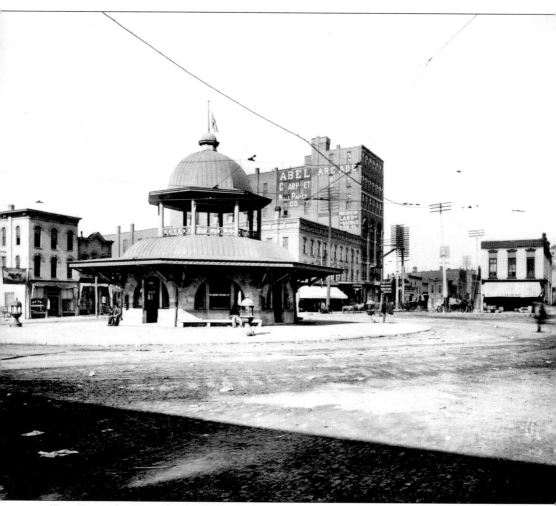

THE TRANSFER HOUSE. This photo was taken a few years after the construction of the Transfer House in 1892. The domed, octagonal structure was originally used by streetcar riders and later by customers of the Interurban or Illinois Traction Railroad. It stood in the center of Lincoln Square until 1962, when it was trucked to its present location in Central Park. The Transfer House has literally and symbolically become the logo for the city, and it remains the single most photographed historical building. It serves as a benchmark for all the changes that surrounded it for over a century. The cityscape, the clothing styles, and the vehicular traffic are a little different in every single picture. (Courtesy Decatur Public Library.)

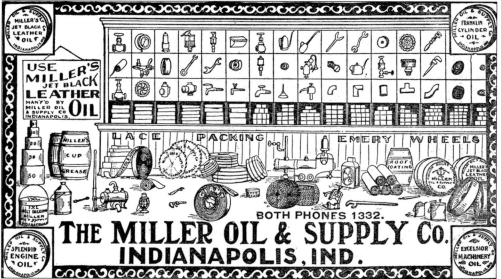

BUSINESS CARD OF FRANK BENCH. At the turn of the century, Frank Bench, a "commercial traveler" or traveling salesman, served as an agent for the Miller Oil Company of Indiana, which is still in existence today. In 1901, Mr. Branch resided at 865 West Pugh Street. He sold hardware, tarpaper, and the special oil used on the industrial belts of the period. Factories were powered by these belts, so keeping them in good operating order was essential. Hundreds of these belts were humming on any given day in Decatur during the early years of the 20th century. (Courtesy of the author.)

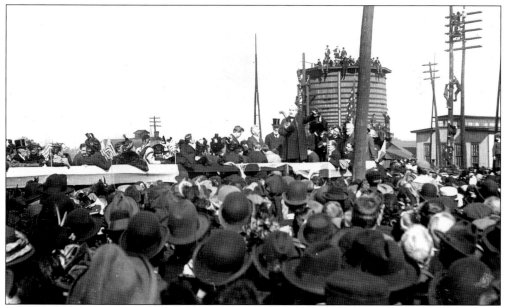

PRESIDENT WILLIAM B. MCKINLEY. President McKinley is shown giving a speech on October 15, 1898. McKinley is the white-haired gentleman standing in the center to the right of the man with the black top hat. He is speaking on the platform of the Wabash Railroad. Other presidents who visited Decatur include Lincoln, Teddy and Franklin Roosevelt, Taft, Truman, Eisenhower, Kennedy, and Reagan. (Courtesy Decatur Public Library.)

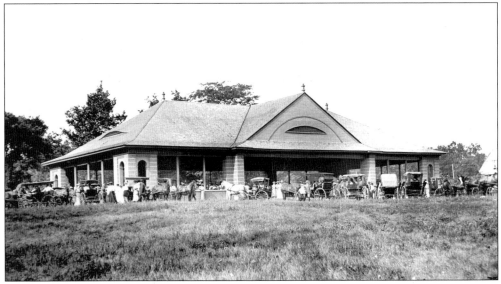

FAIRVIEW PARK PAVILION. This turn-of-the-century scene shows families enjoying a picnic in Fairview Park, just before the automobile era began. The long, low-slung pavilion building is a natural precursor of the Prairie Style soon to be championed by architect Frank Lloyd Wright. Picnics and family reunions have long been rituals of Midwestern family life. (Courtesy Decatur Public Library.)

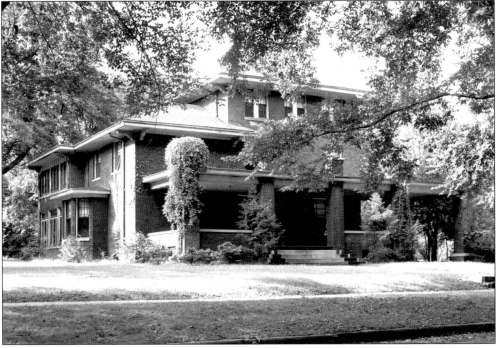

THOMAS T. ROBERTS HOUSE. This handsome home at 919 West William Street was photographed in 1904. It is another example of a kind of "folk" Prairie Style, with its emphasis on broad, horizontal lines inspired by the grand, sweeping prairie. It is located about a block northwest of the James Millikin Homestead. (Courtesy Decatur Public Library.)

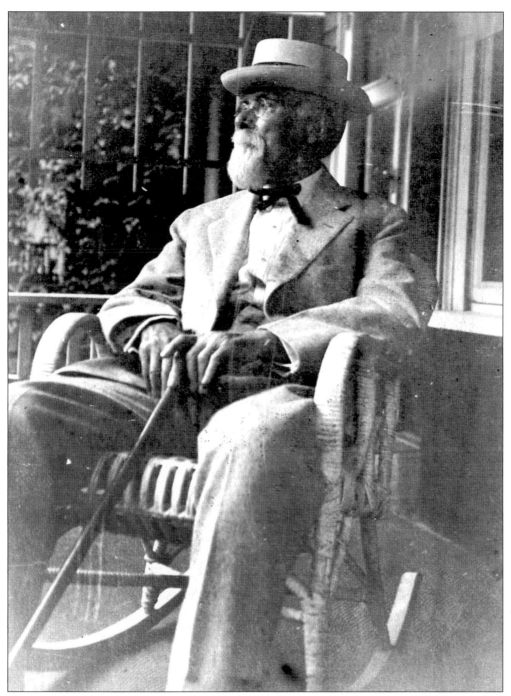

PORTRAIT OF THOMAS T. ROBERTS. Thomas T. Roberts was born March 1, 1839, and died November 11, 1919. This photo is dated March 2, 1919, and was taken on the front porch of the Roberts' home on West William Street. T.T. Roberts was one of the "movers and shakers" in Old Decatur, a wealthy industrialist and philanthropist who made his money as founder of the Decatur Coffin Company. He was an active member of the First Presbyterian Church and a proud Civil War veteran. (Courtesy Decatur Public Library.)

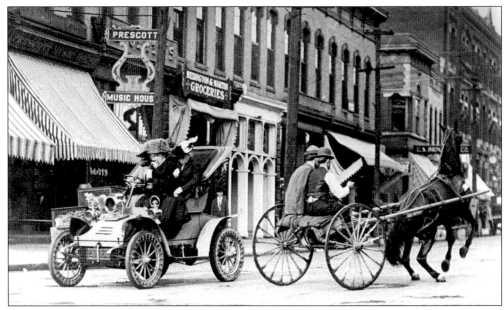

HORSE VS. AUTOMOBILE. In this photograph, taken in 1905, an early automobile frightens a horse pulling two men on a simple cart. Although the cars were noisy and left trails of pollution, the same charges could be leveled at their equine predecessors. Note the music and grocery stores in the background. The fancy striped canvas awnings over many shop fronts suggest that 1905 was a good year for business. (Courtesy Macon County Historical Society.)

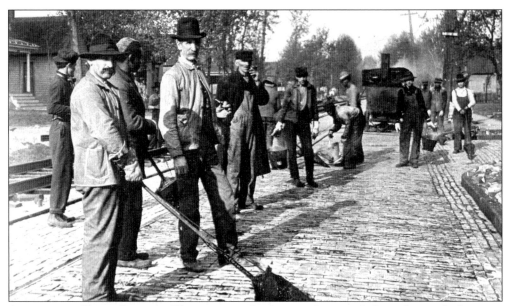

ASPHALTING BRICK STREETS. These city workers are applying asphalt to the cracks between the bricks around the turn of the century. Wooden blocks were also used for paving until concrete or asphalt became the norm in the 1920s. African-American workers are part of the street crew. Although there were free African-Americans in Decatur before the Civil War, immigration from the south (Tennessee and Mississippi in particular) continued through the World War II era. (Courtesy Macon County Historical Society.)

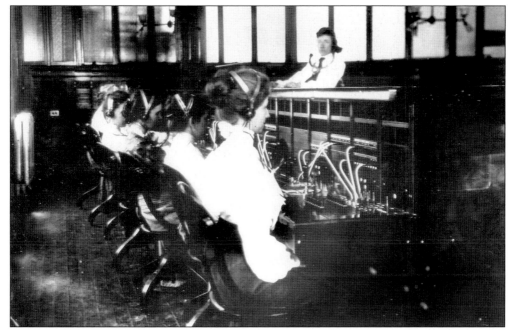

SWITCHBOARD OPERATORS. Decatur did not wait for the time of "Rosie the Riveter" to employ women, as they were certainly part of the workforce from post-Civil War days and afterward, particularly in the many garment factories. But they did many other jobs, as these 1904 switchboard operators demonstrate at the Central Union Telephone Company office. (Courtesy Decatur Public Library.)

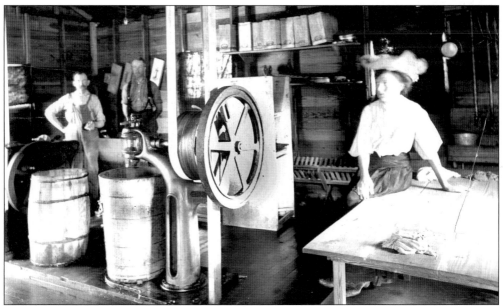

HIGH ICE CREAM. Workers pose at the David High Ice Cream Company around 1900. Note the leather belt supplying power to the mixing barrels . It is unclear whether the young woman in the furred or feathered hat wore her chapeau every day or was simply striking a special pose for the unknown photographer. (Courtesy Decatur Public Library.)

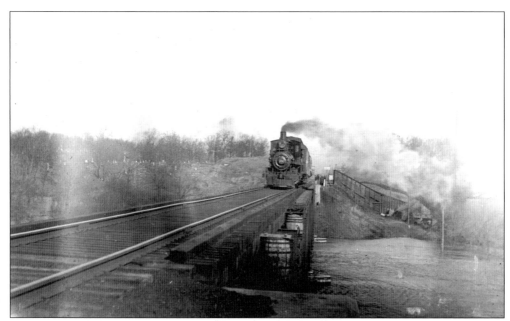

INDIANAPOLIS, DECATUR & SRINGFIELD RY.

DECATUR ROUTE.

PULLMAN COMBINED SLEEPING and RECLINING CHAIR CARS

Between COLUMBUS and PEORIA

via Pan Handle, I., D. & S. and P., D. & E. Rys.

RECLINING CHAIR CARS

Between CINCINNATI and PEORIA

via C., H. & D.. I., D. & S. and P., D. & E. Rys.

And between INDIANAPOLIS and KEOKUK

via I., D., & S. and W., St. L. & P Rys.

TO QUINCY AND HANNIBAL WITHOUT LEAVING THE TRAIN.

THE SHORTEST POSSIBLE ROUTE BETWEEN THE EAST AND WEST.

C. W. BENDER,
Superintendent.

JNO. S. LAZARUS,
Gen'l Pass. Agt.

TICKET POUCH. This little envelope held Wabash Railroad tickets for the Decatur Route, dated about 1905. A kind of mythology or legendary aura grew up around the railroads in America, and they became the subject of many folk songs and paintings. Collecting railroad memorabilia was already a passion by the time of the Civil War, and Decatur quickly embraced the Wabash and all its artifacts. Many famous Wabash trains came through Decatur, and for a time the city served as headquarters to the company. (Courtesy of Patrick Riley.)

ILLINOIS CENTRAL LOCOMOTIVE. This onrushing train was photographed on January 20, 1907, by J.K. Stafford. The negative was part of a collection stored in an attic until July 1953, when discovered by Jack French of Cerro Gordo, Illinois, who then donated the images to the local history room of the Decatur Public Library. (Courtesy Decatur Public Library.)

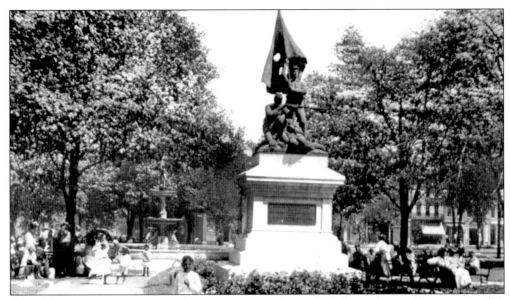

GAR MONUMENT. This postcard commemorates the newly dedicated monument, on April 6, 1905, to the Union dead in the Civil War. Although Decatur boasts quite a few statues, this grouping in bronze may well be the most handsome. It is difficult to imagine Central Park without this landmark. This picture is one of the earliest in the Decatur archives to show children and adults relaxing and having a good time in nice weather. (Courtesy Patrick Riley.)

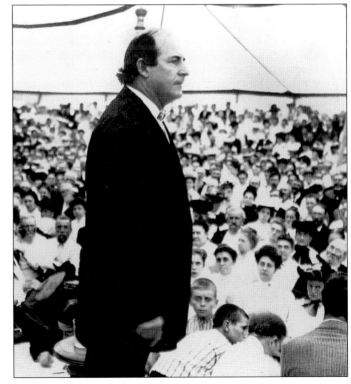

WILLIAM JENNINGS BRYAN. This stereograph was intended for a use in a stereoscope, a kind of early "Viewmaster," very popular in the early 20th century. Bryan spoke at a 1905 Chautaqua meeting in Decatur on his favorite theme, "The Cross of Gold" Stereograph by C.L. Wasson, considered one of the masters of early American photography. (Courtesy Patrick Riley.)

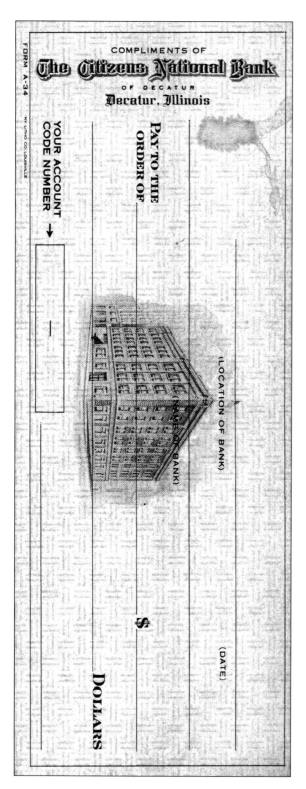

BLANK COUNTER CHECK. This counter check from the Citizens National Bank dates to about 1910. Decatur was an important town for banking, as large amounts of capital flowed in and out of the city as the industries expanded, buying and selling more products. Important bankers include J. Peddecord, Lowber Burrows, Orville B. Gorin, and James Millikin. Aside from the Citizens Bank, the important institutions were the First National Bank and the Millikin Bank, now Union Planters. (Courtesy Decatur Public Library.)

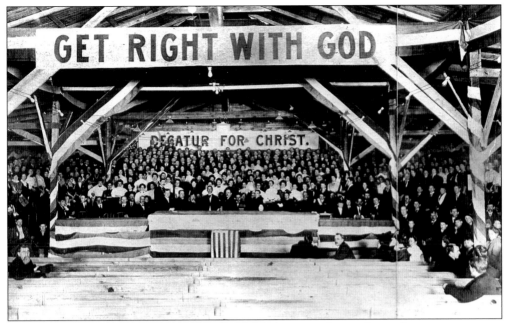

BILLY SUNDAY REVIVAL. Billy Sunday, the fiery, white-suited revival preacher, was in town on February 9, 1908. He was the most famous evangelist of his day, and the packed building attests to his popularity with the local audience. (Courtesy Patrick Riley.)

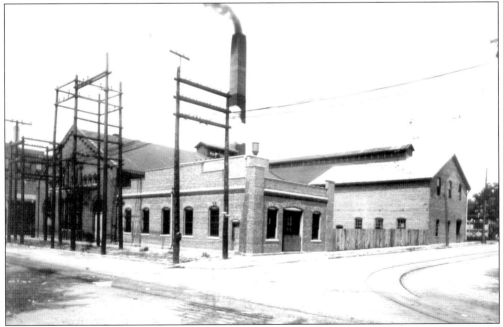

ELECTRIC POWER PLANT. The Decatur Railway and Light Company generated electricity at this plant downtown, which provided power for the electric streetcars and all the light bulbs in the city, as well as many industrial applications. A new smokestack was added shortly after this photo was taken on April 18, 1909. This plant later became part of Illinois Power Company. (Courtesy Decatur Public Library.)

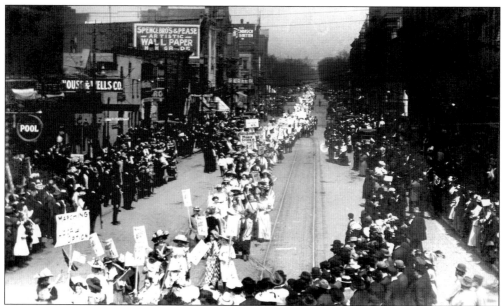

WOMEN'S TEMPERANCE DEMONSTRATION. In 1910, a year that Billy Sunday also gave temperance sermons in Decatur, these ladies marched downtown, chanting, "Less Booze, More Shoes." The sign at the head of the parade reads "Marching for Local Option." And Decatur did briefly opt to prohibit liquor, although this "dry" ordinance flew in the face of the city's history and tradition and did not last very long. (Courtesy Patrick Riley.)

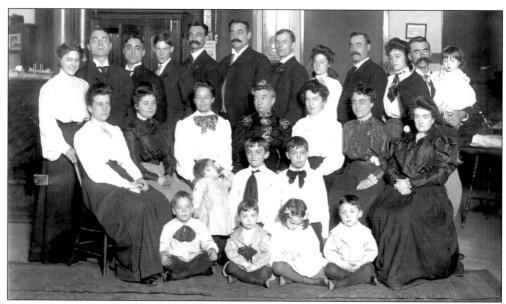

MUELLER FAMILY PORTRAIT. Taken on January 8, 1905, this is a group photo of the Hieronymus Mueller Family taken about five years after the patriarch's death. Mrs. Mueller is sitting in the very center in a dark dress, below the face of the grandfather clock. On the far left is her granddaughter, Clara, who breaks with portrait tradition and smiles broadly. All the Mueller children and grandchildren, save two, are present in this sitting. The photo was taken by the Vandeventer Studio of Decatur. (Courtesy Decatur Public Library.)

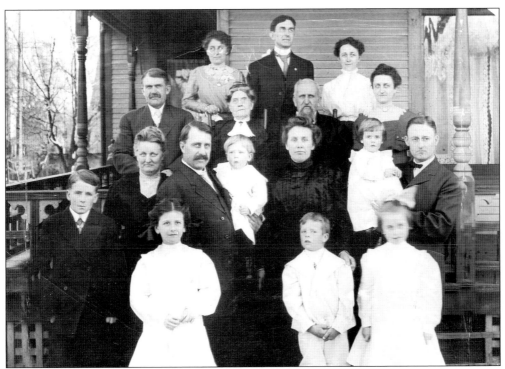

ARCHER T. DAVIS FAMILY. At this family reunion, Mrs. and Mrs. A.T. Davis (the elderly couple sitting at the top center and back of the group) had the pleasure of seeing their entire clan gathered together on a March day in 1910. He was a Decatur druggist. The grandchild on the bottom right managed to turn her head at exactly the wrong moment, and the lady on the top left is looking off in the distance. The trees had not yet begun to bud. (Courtesy Decatur Public Library.)

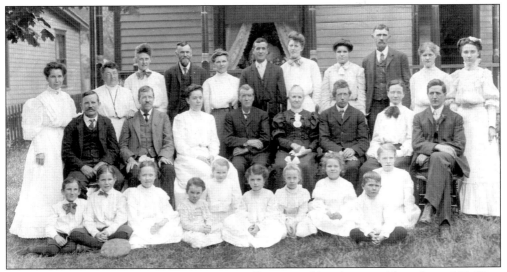

THE EDGAR R. KELLINGTON FAMILY. E.R. Kellington sold and repaired bicycles at 223 West William Street. This family was an ordinary, middle-class group that obviously held tenaciously to family values, as did all the residents of Decatur in 1904, when this group portrait was taken. (Courtesy Decatur Public Library.)

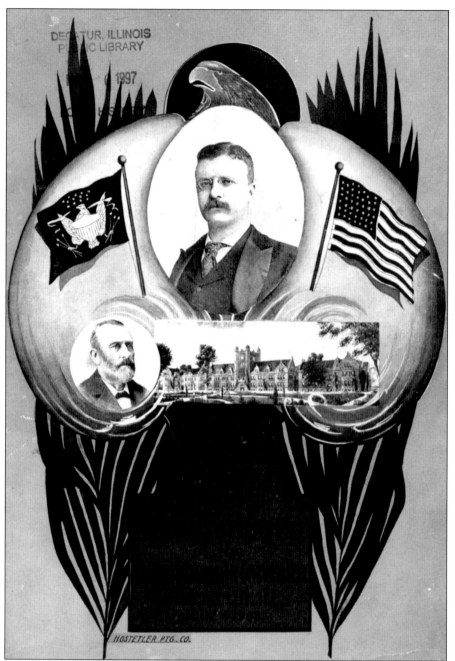

DEDICATION OF MILLIKIN UNIVERSITY. This graphic shows the cover of the program booklet for the dedication of Millikin University on June 4, 1903. President Theodore Roosevelt, then on a campaign tour, was persuaded to give the dedicatory speech. Ever reticent, James Millikin deliberately stayed in the background, even though it was his triumphant day. The inset illustrations show Roosevelt, Millikin himself, and the three original buildings of the university, now joined together. Roosevelt made a few remarks when he arrived at the Wabash Station in Decatur, then apparently took the Illinois Central line (which still runs due east of the University), made a special stop, and delivered his speech. (Courtesy Decatur Public Library.)

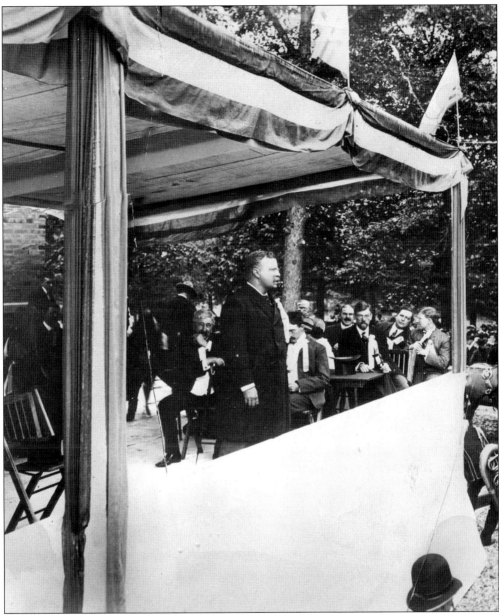

THEODORE ROOSEVELT. Roosevelt appears to be watching the band members on the day of the dedication of Millikin University, June 4, 1903. He is shown standing on the speaker's platform with other dignitaries—the general audience is in the deep background. Roosevelt was one of the most famous men in America at this time, not merely as a President but also as the leader of the "Rough Riders" in the Spanish-American War of 1898. The University was fortunate to land a man of his stature, and Roosevelt was delighted to have another audience. (Courtesy Millikin University.)

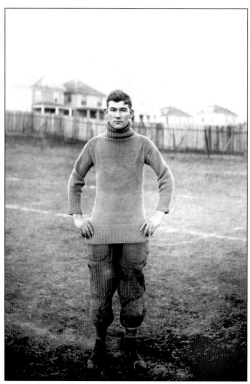

PETE GOOD. Pete Good served as a substitute end on the Millikin football squad of 1910. The amount and quality of equipment (helmets, shoulder pads, etc.) varied from game to game. The emphasis seemed to be on having a good time. (Courtesy Decatur Public Library.)

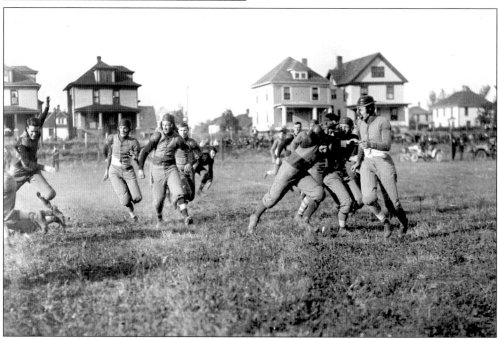

MILLIKIN VS. NORMAL. In this October 1908 encounter, there is action on the gridiron as Millikin encounters its rival, Normal (now Illinois State University). At the moment the photograph was shot, Millikin was winning 8-2. Today, Millikin has a modern playing field and bleachers, and the players wear considerably upgraded gear. (Courtesy Decatur Public Library.)

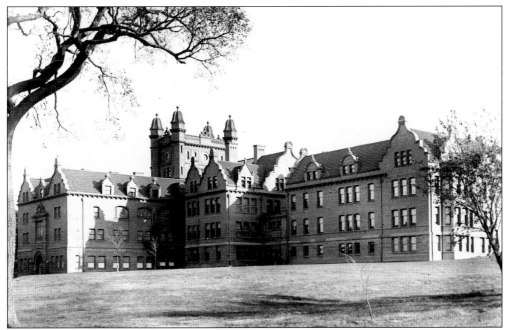

MILLIKIN UNIVERSITY. This view shows the back of Millikin University in the afternoon shadows about 1908. In today's landscape, the photographer would be standing on the open ground between Gorin Hall and the Staley Library. This photo highlights the "tulips" on the Millikin tower and other distinctive features of the Dutch Baroque architecture, which was executed from local bricks fired in a special kiln on the ground where the Alpha Chi Omega House stands today on Oakland Avenue (Route 48). (Courtesy Decatur Public Library.)

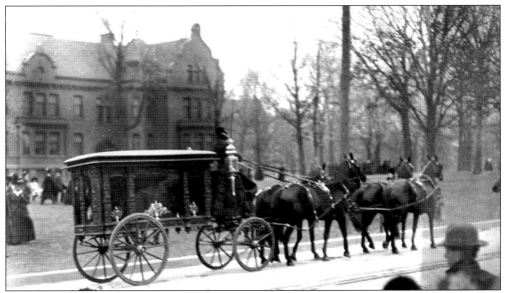

FUNERAL PROCESSION. James Millikin was buried on the cold snowy day of March 6, 1909. In this photo, the students have turned out to pay their respects to the man who made their education possible. Even today, Millikin still helps through the Millikin Foundation. (Courtesy Decatur Public Library.)

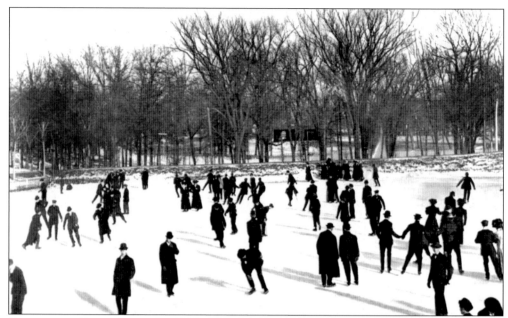

SKATERS IN DREAMLAND. In 1908, the skaters in Dreamland Amusement Park were very nicely attired, in spite of the chilly temperatures. Dreamland was part of a 10-acre tract that was added to the rest of Fairview Park in 1919. (Courtesy Decatur Public Library.)

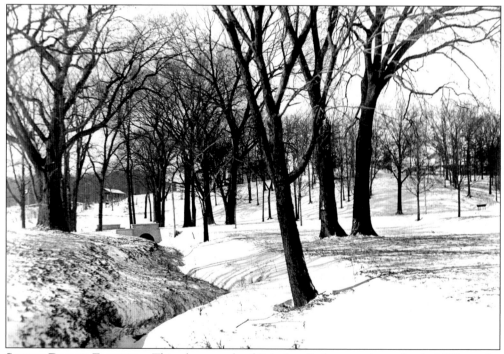

SNOWY DAY IN FAIRVIEW. This photograph of Fairview Park on a winter day in 1909 exudes a dreamy, poetic quality, with bare trees leaving pencil-thin shadows on the snow-dusted ground. This part of the park remains nearly the same almost a century later. (Courtesy Decatur Public Library.)

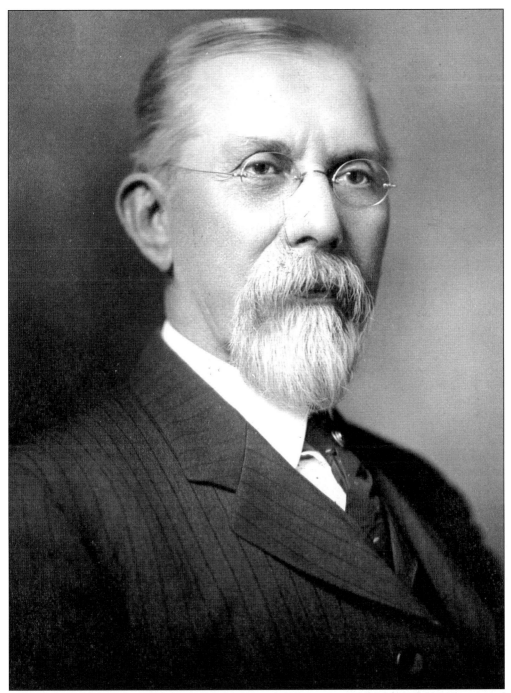

Portrait of David S. Shellabarger. Decatur industrial pioneer D.S. Shellabarger posed for this formal portrait taken by the Vandeventer Studio on January 7, 1912, about a year before his death on January 2, 1913. He began milling grain in Decatur as early as 1856, but he sold his mills to the American Hominy Company in 1892. Later, he organized the Shellabarger Elevator Co., served as president of the National Bank, and finally as president of the Manufacturers and Consumers' Coal Company. (Courtesy Decatur Public Library.)

51

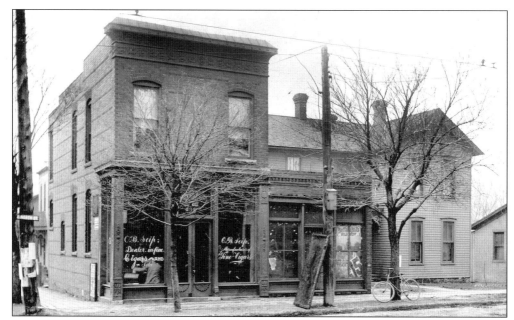

SEIPS CIGAR STORE. Oliver B. Seips was one of about 400 men in Decatur engaged in the rolling of fine cigars. Seips also was a "dealer in fine cigars and tobaccos," competing with more upscale establishments like Michl's Cigar Store downtown. This photo, taken in the late winter of 1909 by George Baker, shows a customer having a smoke in Seips' store at 439 East North. His residence was one block south at 427 East William. (Courtesy Decatur Public Library.)

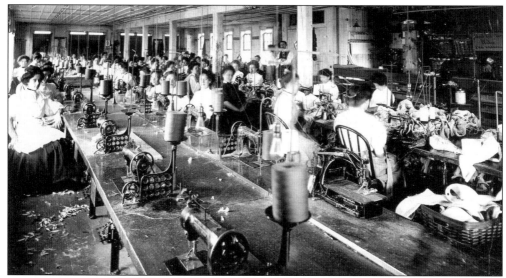

MUHLENBRUCH GLOVE CO. Unlike cigar-rolling, which was definitely considered a man's work, glove-making fell under the sphere of women's activities. Garment-making in general was part of the Decatur manufacturing scene for about 100 years, from, say, 1880 to 1980. Clearly, women have always been a major contributor to the prosperity of the city. The photo is dated September 13, 1908. (Courtesy Decatur Public Library.)

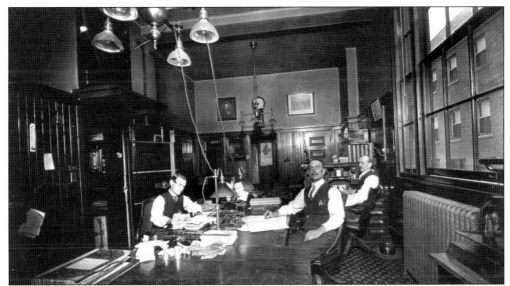

POST OFFICE WORKERS. In this interior shot, post office employees are busy at work in their new building, around 1910. Picture, from left to right, are Fred W. Gray, W.W. Kyle, and Assistant Postmaster Fred C. Stoewsand. Electric cords are connected to the light fixture overhead and left dangling over the work table. (Courtesy Decatur Public Library.)

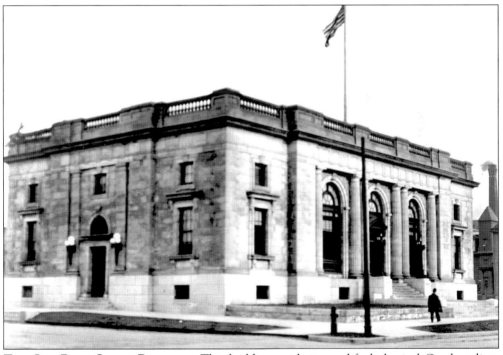

THE OLD POST OFFICE BUILDING. This building, with its modified classical Greek styling, stood at the corner of Main and Eldorado Streets from 1909 to 1935, when the present downtown post office was built on Franklin Street. The Carnegie Library was directly across the street to the west. Both buildings were important city landmarks for decades. (Courtesy Decatur Public Library.)

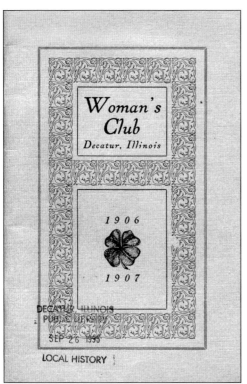

DECATUR WOMAN'S CLUB. This little artifact from 1906 is a concrete example of the active involvement of women in Decatur's cultural and social life. Women's clubs were especially visible during the World War I era when women organized food drives, made bandages, and otherwise contributed to the war effort. And they kept meticulous records of their activities, saving menus, cancelled checks, and other pertinent documents. (Courtesy Decatur Public Library.)

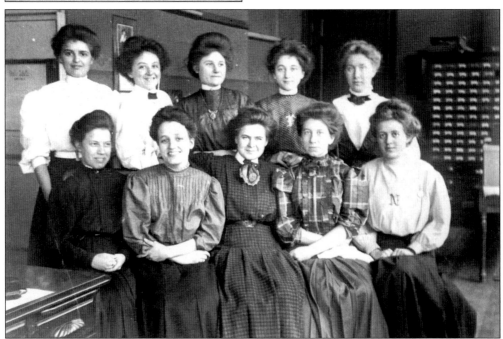

TELEPHONE OPERATORS. In the previous decade, women's fashions and deportments had begun to break away from the strict standards of Victorian propriety. This photo, from about 1915, shows a group of telephone operators dressed in a variety of outfits and hairstyles—and most of the ladies are actually smiling. (Courtesy Decatur Public Library.)

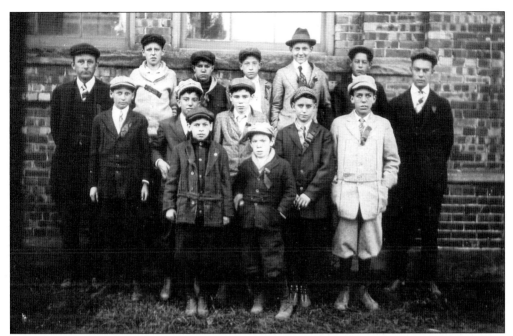

DECATUR NEWSBOYS. This group photo of 1916 shows unidentified newspaper carriers from the *Decatur Review* sporting the latest fashions and enjoying themselves at the Illinois State Fair in Springfield. In the very next year, America would send the American Expeditionary Force (AEF) to fight in France. (Courtesy Decatur Public Library.)

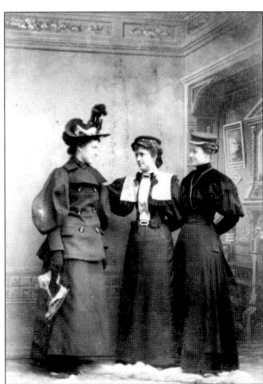

A TRIO OF LADIES. These three unidentified ladies, obviously friends, visited the East End Gallery at 1079 East Eldorado Street and posed in front of a backdrop for this photo, taken about 1915. The first jazz records would soon appear on the scene, ushering in the decade of the 1920s. Perhaps these darkly clad ladies might well have become "flapper girls" a few years later, as dance fads like the Charleston swept the nation. (Courtesy Decatur Public Library.)

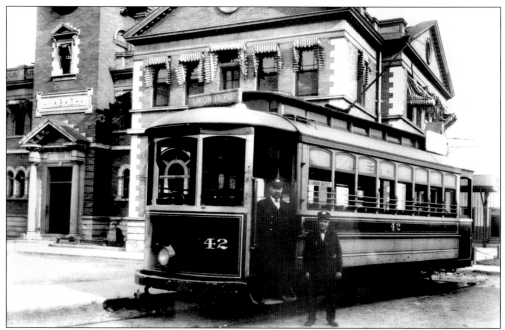

STREETCAR NO. 42. The electric streetcar was widely used in Decatur at this time, about 1915. The photo shows Streetcar No. 42, with its driver and ticket-taker. The vehicle was on the "Union Depot" route and had properly come to rest in front of the Wabash Station seen in the background. (Courtesy Decatur Public Library.)

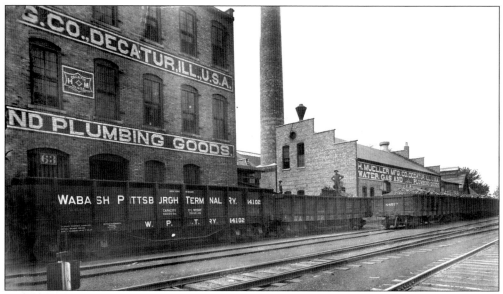

MUELLER COMPANY. The Mueller Company and various breakaway companies, like Cash Valve and Cashco, created a deep infrastructure of parts, raw materials, suppliers, and skilled workers that made Decatur valves competitive, high-quality products recognized nationally and internationally. Taken about 1915, this shot illustrates the symbiosis between the railroads and industry (here, Wabash and Mueller). The buildings are on West Cerro Gordo Street. (Courtesy Decatur Public Library.)

MUELLER FAUCET ADVERTISEMENT. This advertisement with the tag line, "Faucets without a Fault," appeared around 1930, and it is directed to the homeowner or builder. The emphasis is on quality and durability. (Courtesy Decatur Public Library.)

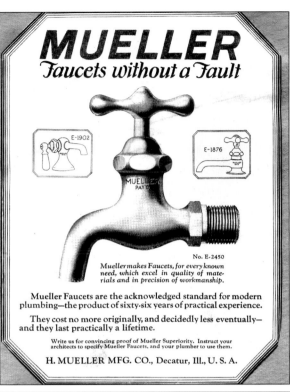

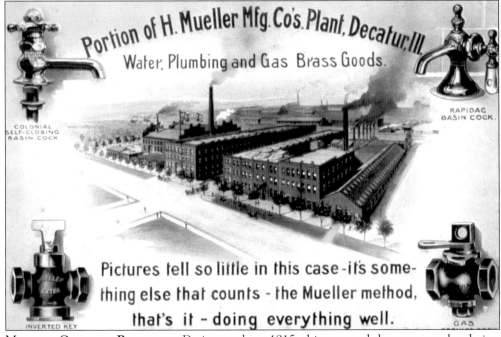

MUELLER COMPANY POSTCARD. Dating to about 1915, this postcard shows an overhead view of the plant, with inset graphics illustrating four of the most popular "brass goods." In an age before heightened environmental consciousness, smokestacks were considered a symbol of industrial wealth. (Courtesy Patrick Riley.)

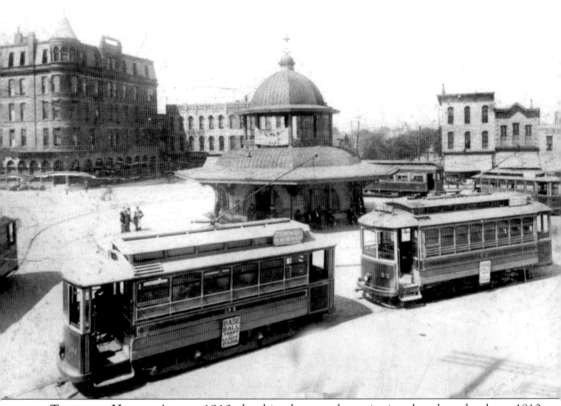

TRANSFER HOUSE, ABOUT 1910. In this photograph, sepia-tinted and made about 1910, posters affixed to sides of streetcars proclaim, "Base Ball Today at League Park." There is also a baseball banner hanging from the clerestory of the Transfer House itself. In the background, at left, stands the Saint Nicholas Hotel and on the very right the "Hue" Singleton Building. The camera is aimed to the southwest. (Courtesy Decatur Public Library.)

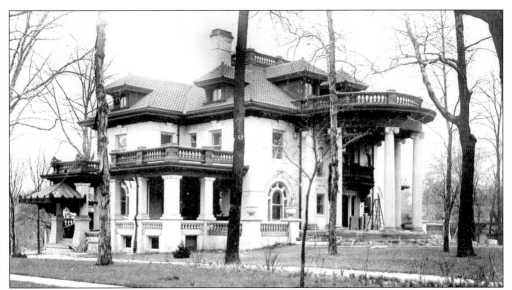

CHARLES G. POWERS MANSION. Built at a cost of over $83,000 in 1910 money, this elegant mansion would probably cost at least one-and-a-half million dollars to build today, with its lavish use of marble, copper guttering, Mediterranean tile, cream colored brick, and mahogany. It is easily the most sumptuous personal residence ever constructed in Decatur. The portico, with is Ionic stone columns, is distinctive, grand, and yet somehow intimate. Charles' son Jack lived in the house for half a century, until 1975. (Courtesy Patrick Riley.)

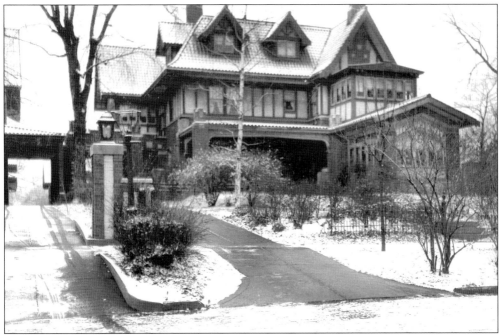

C.E. ENGLAND HOUSE. Originally built in 1882 by W.M. Chambers, the house was extensively remodeled by Charles Edward England in 1916, employing the English Tudor exposed beam and stucco features known locally as "the stick style." This photo was taken on a snowy day, December 9, 1933. (Courtesy Decatur Public Library.)

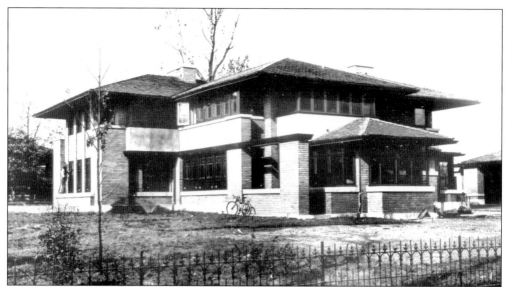

ROBERT MUELLER HOUSE. This modern home at No. 1 Millikin Place, just northeast of the James Millikin Homestead, is part of a trio usually labeled the "Frank Lloyd Wright houses," which is only partly true. Although all three homes (No. 1, No. 2, and No. 4 Millikin Place) bear Wright's distinctive stylistic matrix, only No. 1 carries a Wright signature on its documentation . All three were, in fact, completed by Wright's most trusted subalterns, Marion Mahony and Walter Burley Griffin. Photo taken about 1912. (Courtesy Decatur Public Library.)

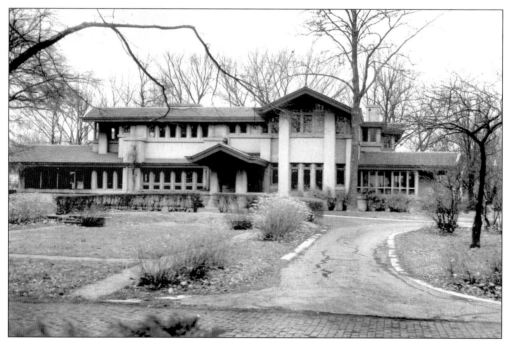

ADOLPH MUELLER HOUSE. This lovely structure, with its strong Japanese rooflines, was built in 1911 by Charles Mueller, later owned by Adolph Mueller. In the 1990s, it was used as the presidential residence by two Millikin University presidents, Curtis McCray and Thomas Flynn. (Courtesy Decatur Public Library.)

60

DECATUR VIEWS. In this 1910 postcard, the viewer sees the following at top left: Water Street, the Transfer House, the GAR Monument, Wabash Station, old high school, old log courthouse, downtown, the Carnegie Library, Fairview Park, and Millikin University. (Courtesy Patrick Riley.)

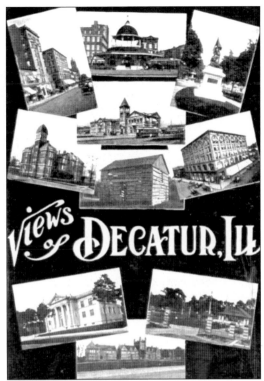

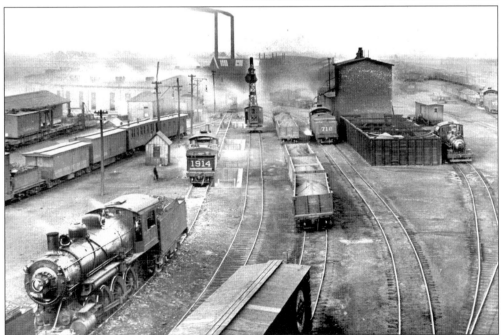

ILLINOIS CENTRAL REPAIR YARDS. Taken on May 17, 1910, this photograph shows the roundhouse and repair yards of the Illinois Central Railroad in Clinton, just north of Decatur. This repair facility still exists today. The railroads have always been at the center of the economic life of Decatur; everything else depended upon them. (Courtesy Decatur Public Library.)

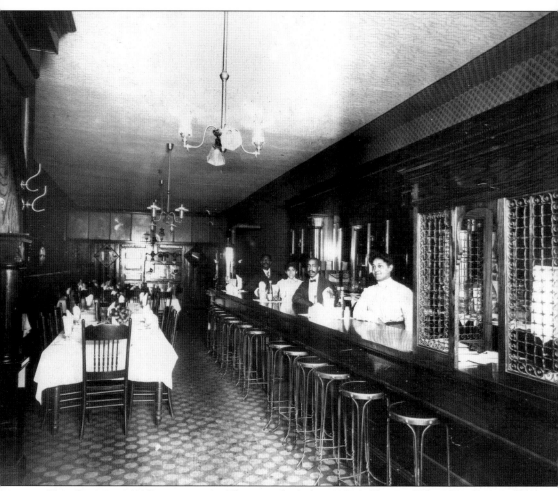

HUE SINGLETON'S RESTAURANT. Photographed about 1910, Huston "Hue" Singleton and his wife Laura proudly show off their famous restaurant and chop house, which operated successfully on the northwest side of Lincoln Square from 1901 to 1919. Singleton came to Decatur from Iowa around the turn of the century, quickly going into business for himself after some local hotel work. Hue Singleton was the first important African-American entrepreneur in Decatur, well respected and affluent. He built a home on McKinley on the north side of the city. Around 1922, after he had retired from business, the City Directory suddenly affixed the racial designation "col" (for "colored") after his name, a reflection of the isolationist, anti-immigrant feelings that welled up nationally after World War I. Also, Decatur did briefly have a Klan chapter in the early 1920s, which fortunately disappeared. In this connection it is worth noting that African-American Samuel Bush was hanged from a light post on June 6, 1893, for apparently molesting a Caucasian woman in Mt. Zion. The charge was never proved, but the incident mobilized the African-American community and later helped to create the first chapter of the NAACP in the city. (Courtesy Decatur Public Library.)

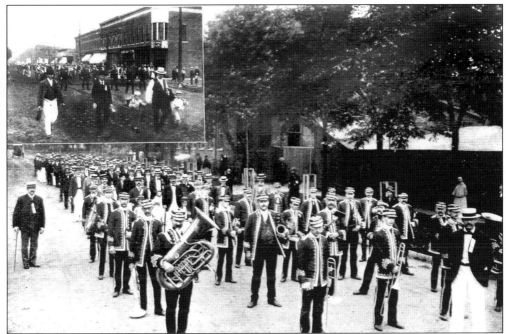

DECATUR MUNICIPAL BAND. Known originally as the Goodman Band, after its charismatic director Andrew Goodman, the Decatur Municipal Band has been in continual existence since its founding in 1857. The band still plays free summer concerts for the citizenry. This photo, with the inset of the band marching, dates to about 1910. (Courtesy Decatur Public Library.)

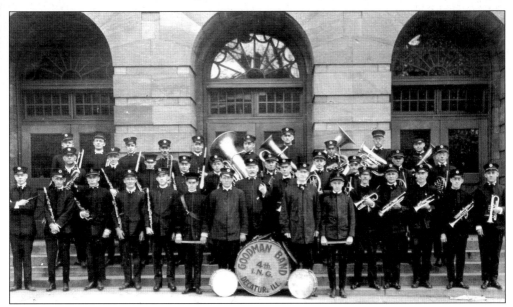

FORMAL PORTRAIT OF THE GOODMAN BAND. Bands became extremely popular during and after the Civil War, band uniforms undoubtedly being part of the attraction. The Goodman Band seems to have changed the style of theirs about every five years or so. Bands typically played patriotic songs, marches, and some of the hit tunes of the day, like "A Bicycle Built for Two" or "Pretty Baby." (Courtesy Decatur Public Library.)

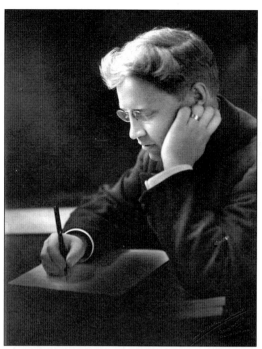

PROFESSOR HAROLD A. COLE. In this artistic and well-lit portrait taken about 1912, Millikin University Professor Harold A. Cole works over a musical score. He taught piano and organ and was a graduate of the New England Conservatory of Music in Boston, Massachusetts. Cole must have brought a considerable amount of culture to the little town on the prairie, which, like Millikin, placed a high value on musical expression of all kinds. (Courtesy Decatur Public Library.)

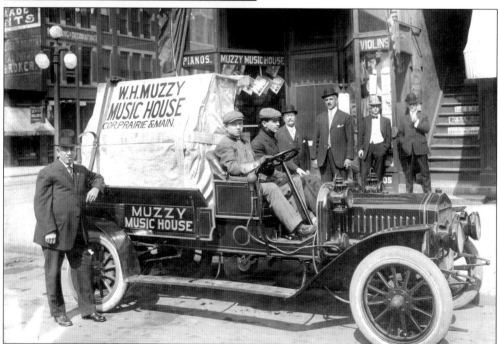

MUZZY MUSIC HOUSE. William H. Muzzy leans against his delivery truck on a sunny day about 1915. A piano is wrapped in canvas and belted down in the bed of the truck. William Muzzy was a dealer in pianos, player pianos, Victor Victrolas, violins, and sheet music—and he did a thriving business in this musically-oriented community. Muzzy's business was at the corner of East Prairie and Main, and he kept an apartment in the nearby Pasfield Building. (Courtesy Decatur Public Library.)

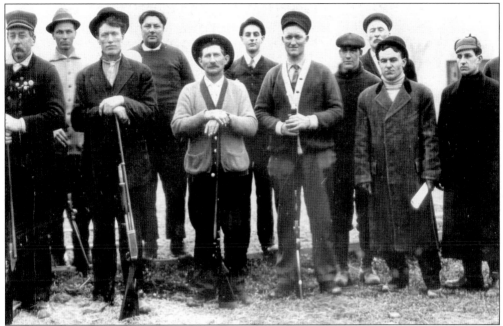

DECATUR GUN CLUB. This photo of the Decatur Gun Club, taken about 1910–1915, may have been taken south of the Sangamon River, which was still largely wooded country with a few hunting lodges and cabins. Decatur abounded in clubs of all kinds for the next half-century. One of the club members on the right is wearing a Sherlock Holmes-style Deerstalker hat. (Courtesy Decatur Public Library.)

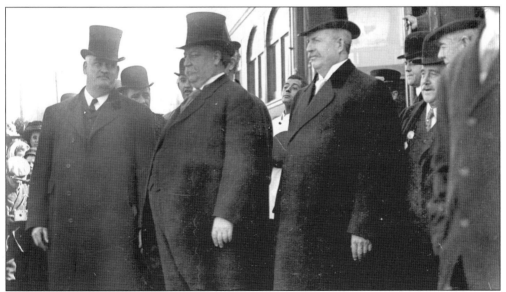

PRESIDENT WILLIAM HOWARD TAFT. President Taft made a brief appearance in Decatur on February 11, 1911. This shot was apparently taken at the Union Depot on a fairly warm day, judging from the attire of the crowd in the background. The president is the large man in the center with the prominent mustache. He weighed about 375 pounds at the time. The other gentlemen in the silk top hats are unidentified. (Courtesy Decatur Public Library.)

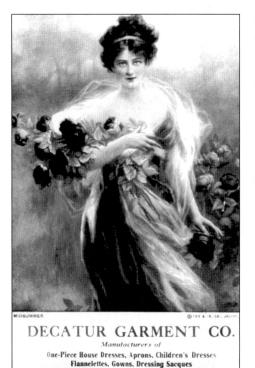

MIDSUMMER

DECATUR GARMENT CO.

Manufacturers of

**One-Piece House Dresses, Aprons, Children's Dresses
Flannelettes, Gowns, Dressing Sacques
and Kimonas**

802-804 N. Water St.   DECATUR, ILL.

DECATUR GARMENT COMPANY. This postcard, dated May 6, 1913, shows a young woman in a rather daring hairstyle and décolletage—not the sort of outfit actually purveyed by the company, which sold, among other items, something called a dressing sacque. This garment was apparently a short dressing-gown or jacket-like robe to be worn while fixing the hair or applying makeup. For a while it seemed as if Decatur would focus on garment-making, rather than becoming a heavy industrial and agribusiness center. The last garment plant did not close its doors until the 1980s. (Courtesy Patrick Riley.)

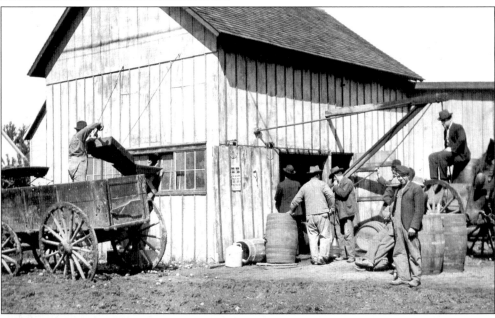

CIDER MILL. Albert Manecke ran this cider mill at the northwest corner of Main and Harrison, suggesting how any organic products were always potentially part of the processing capabilities of the city. Note the absence of any gasoline-powered vehicles, as well as the mud-caked wagon wheels. Manecke lived fairly close to his mill at 2193 North Main. The gentleman in the wagon is apparently unloading apples to be pressed, since the photo was taken September 24, 1911, in high season. (Courtesy Decatur Public Library.)

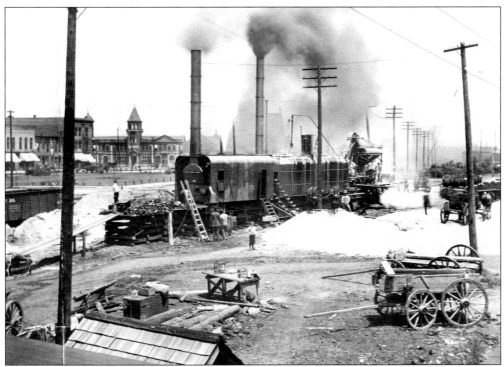

STREICHER'S ASPHALT PLANT. The very existence of the plant in this photo, taken in November 1911, suggests the economic vitality of the city. Asphalt was used in many ways, including patching the endless potholes in brick streets. The Model-T had been introduced three years earlier by Henry Ford in Detroit, but no automobiles of any kind are visible. The Wabash Depot is in the background at left. (Courtesy Decatur Public Library.)

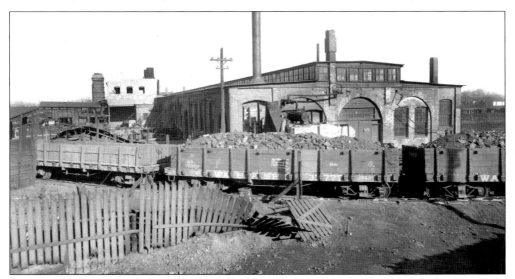

CENTRAL MALLEABLE IRON CO. From this foundry came the rails, sheets, and other metal products that literally fed the other industries in Decatur, as the railroad fed the Central Malleable Iron Company itself. The hopper cars are apparently bringing in a load of ore, possibly from the Minnesota iron range. (Courtesy Decatur Public Library.)

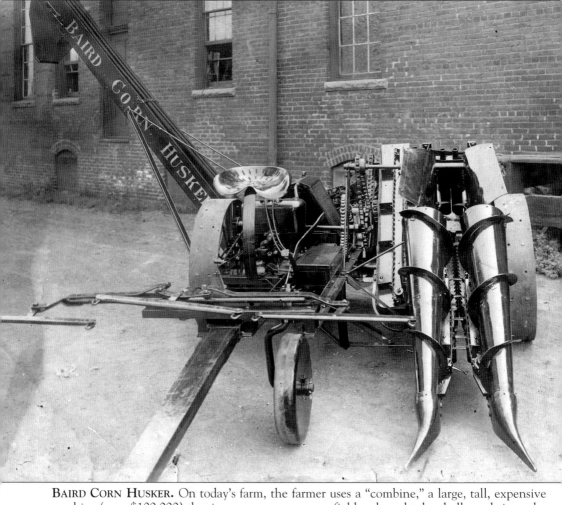

BAIRD CORN HUSKER. On today's farm, the farmer uses a "combine," a large, tall, expensive machine (over $100,000) that in one pass over a corn field gathers, husks, shells, and ejects the grain into a suitable bin or wagon. All those operations had to be invented singly—and that entire process happened in Decatur. In addition, the check-row planter was invented in Decatur, too, allowing the planting of corn along any axis of an imaginary grid. From that perspective, the GPS (global positioning satellite) farming of today, along with genetically modified seeds, doesn't seem quite that revolutionary. When William S. Baird invented this harvester in 1913, local farmers instantly improved their economic status, even though they were already making profit from previous agricultural inventions. The nearby University of Illinois was also constantly providing new data about improved methods of livestock care and, of course, information about new hybrid seeds. Farmers who used Baird's corn husker had to be very careful of its moving parts and needed a good supply of oil and lubricants to keep these machines in running order. In fact, when automobiles first appeared in large numbers, around 1909, farmers as a class were the largest purchasers, because they were accustomed to gasoline engines and the required lubrication of chain-driven gears. Farmers also needed the transportation as they lived farthest from the city center. And, finally, their large barns made perfect garages. Photo taken October 4, 1914. (Courtesy Decatur Public Library.)

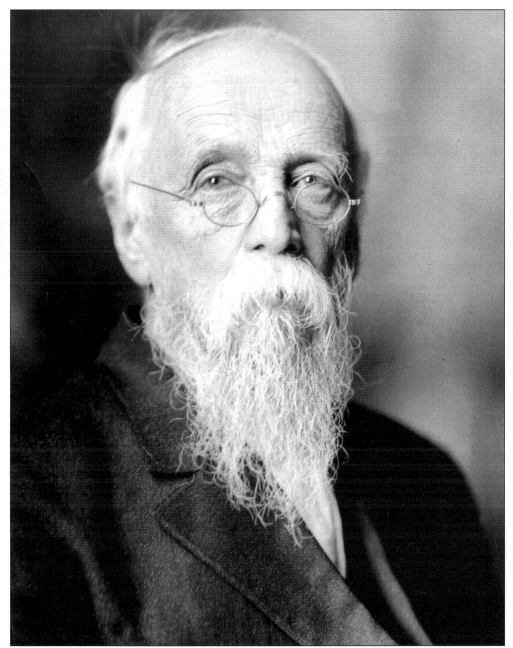

PORTRAIT OF NATHAN L. KRONE. Nathan Krone lived in Decatur from 1839 until his death on March 31, 1916. He had personally witnessed over 75 years of dizzying change in this city on the prairie. Krone spent most of his life downtown as a clerk and then as a druggist. He owned drugstores at Calhoun and Grand, and later at Jasper and East William. Candle-makers in the area suffered a business slump around 1857 when Krone introduced "white oil" (kerosene) in Decatur. Besides patent medicines and other remedies, Krone, like his fellow druggists, sold paint pigments, linseed oil, and other non-pharmaceuticals. By the time of his death, Krone had become something of a living legend and a talkative expert on early Decatur. He was, after all, an eyewitness. Photo by C.L. Wasson in about 1915. (Courtesy Decatur Public Library.)

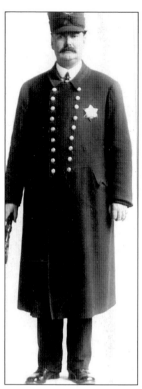

DECATUR POLICEMAN. In this photo by the famed C.L. Wasson, Police Officer Cornelius Doherty, poses with his billy club and large star. This uniform replaced the older "Keystone Cop" look. Doherty served as a police officer for 18 years. He died in 1931. This photo dates to about 1915. (Courtesy Decatur Public Library.)

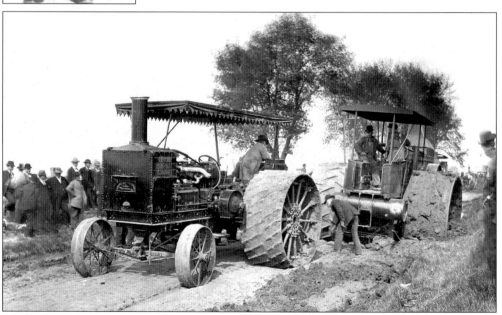

ROAD CONSTRUCTION. Judging from the number of onlookers, road construction provided much-needed entertainment on this otherwise quiet spring day, May 3, 1912. Perhaps the growing population of people—and automobiles—may have spurred road construction. The location and road are not identified, but presumably it was on the edge of the city, since no houses are visible on the horizon. About four decades later, Caterpillar would make some of the best road-grading equipment in the very same city. (Courtesy Decatur Public Library.)

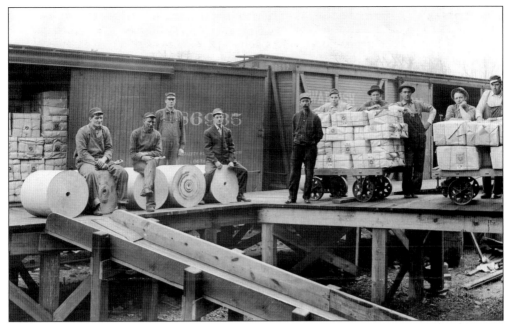

E-Z OPENER BAG COMPANY, FREIGHT DOCK. This photo, taken by George Baker on November 19, 1911, shows workers of the E-Z Opener Bag Company posing next to some of their finished products. The pride in craftsmanship at this time is so high that even the loading dock is beautifully constructed, almost as neatly as a piece of furniture. (Courtesy Decatur Public Library.)

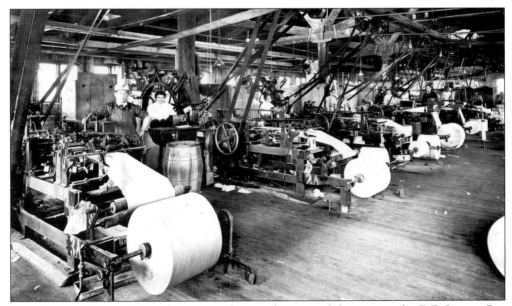

BAG MAKING ROOM. This photo was taken at the original factory site for E-Z Opener Bag Company, at East William and Broadway. The bags were a cheaper and lighter alternative to other containers made of burlap or canvas; they typically held lint, cotton, or other products. E-Z Opener sold them by the thousands. Photo by George Baker, November 19, 1911. (Courtesy Decatur Public Library.)

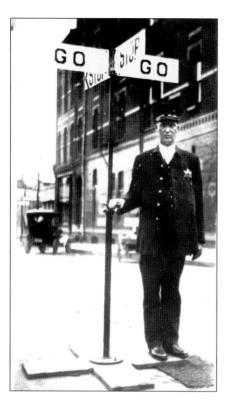

TRAFFIC POLICEMAN. By the time this photo was taken in 1916, the volume of automobile traffic on downtown Decatur streets had increased to the point that traffic semaphores, manually operated by the policemen, were being used at the busiest intersections. Apparently, the cars were slow enough and the drivers courteous enough to insure that the whole system worked. (Courtesy Decatur Public Library.)

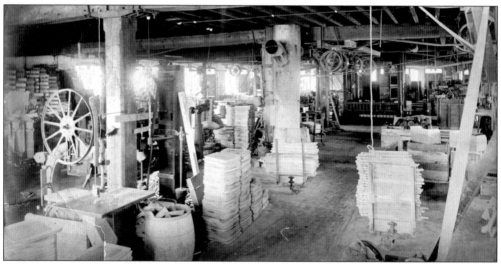

DECATUR CHAIR FACTORY. Decatur was also famed as a furniture manufacturing center, because beds, chests, and chairs were produced here in great quantity. This photograph of the Decatur Chair Factory was taken before the workers were on duty, and the factory floor has an eerie feeling, in spite of the stacks of clean wooden chair backs, bottoms, and rails about to be turned into finished products. The factory was located at 260 North Street. Photo taken about 1910. (Courtesy Decatur Public Library.)

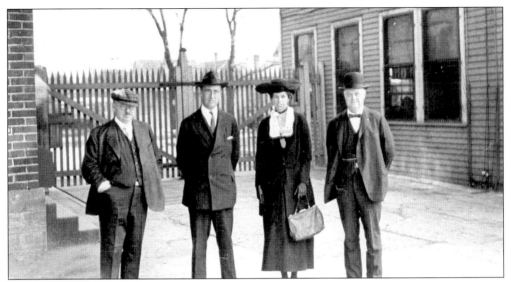

FRANKLIN AND ELEANOR ROOSEVELT. Franklin Roosevelt was visiting Decatur in 1920 on a vice presidential campaign swing, accompanied by his wife Eleanor. On the far right is A.E. Staley and on the far left stands an unidentified gentleman in a natty touring cap. Photo by Rembrandt Studios of Decatur. (Courtesy Decatur Public Library.)

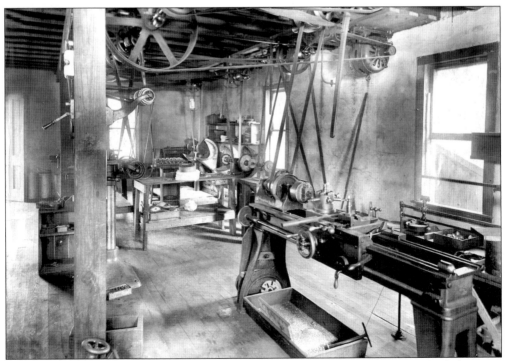

CRUM-WILEY MANUFACTURING COMPANY. These metal lathes produced shafts, bolts, pins, gears, and other key industrial components needed for local consumption or export use. The lathes were powered by overhead electrical motors and the power was then transferred by a series of belts and pulleys to the actual machines on the shop floor. The pan on the floor was a receptacle for cutting oil and metal shavings. (Courtesy Decatur Public Library.)

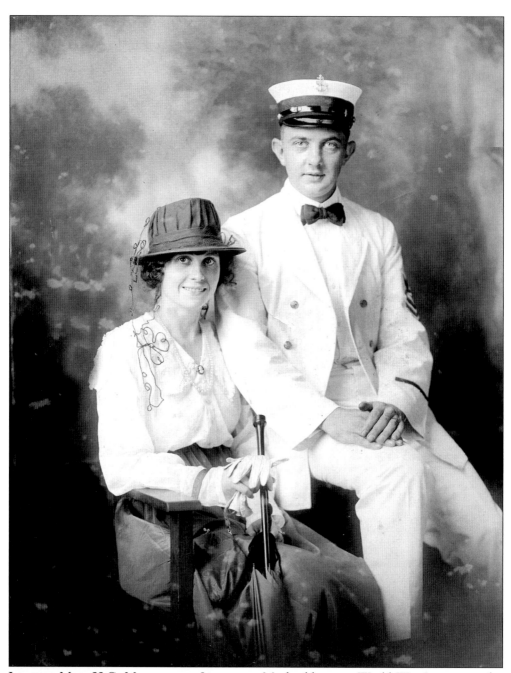

Lt. and Mrs. H.C. Mechtoldt. Lieutenant Mechtoldt was a World War I veteran, who became a career naval officer, serving for several decades. This photograph was taken in 1918 and Mrs. Mechtoldt was wearing the latest in ladies' fashion, including a modern hat with floral veil, gloves, and parasol. The community of Decatur women raised money and helped make bandages for the troops, besides providing a kind of canteen service for all the service men who passed through Decatur's Union Depot. (Courtesy Decatur Public Library.)

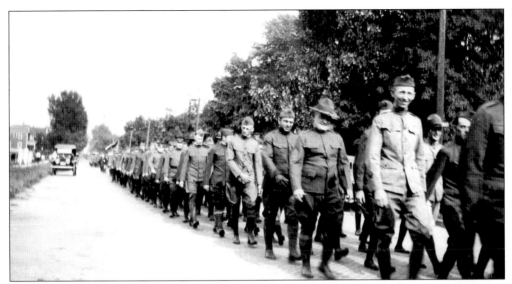

DOUGHBOYS MARCHING. These Decatur veterans are shown marching in Sgt. Castle Williams' funeral procession. In the eulogy, Captain Krigbaum called Williams a "noble soul" who had endured "disease stricken camps, barrage gas attacks, liquid fire squirting, barbed wire entanglements, aeroplane bombing . . . and over-the-top maneuvers." Captain Krigbaum was Castle's commanding officer, and he added that the sergeant always gave him a "ten dollar salute." (Courtesy Decatur Public Library.)

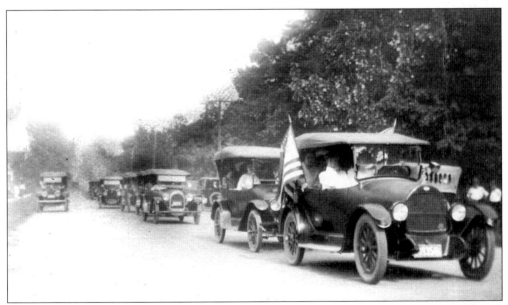

FUNERAL OF SGT. CASTLE WILLIAMS. On July 24, 1921, the remains of Sgt. Castle Williams, whose name is still honored by the local American Legion post, were buried at Fairlawn Cemetery in an elaborate funeral, which began with services at the First Presbyterian Church. Since World War I ended in November 1918, American "doughboys" did not return home via troop ships until 1919—or even 1920. Another Decatur hero from the Great War was Italian-American Sgt. Vito Bertoldo, who did survive and became Decatur's only recipient of the Congressional Medal of Honor. (Courtesy Decatur Public Library.)

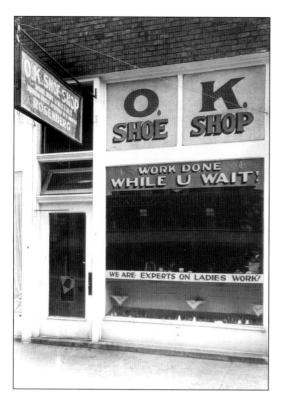

O.K. SHOE SHOP. This 1929 photo of Harry Rosenberg's OK Shoe Hospital is a metaphor for all the other small shops that provided consumer services for the next three decades, the Golden Era of Decatur when doctors still made house calls, milk and ice were delivered to the door, and every neighborhood had its own "mom and pop" grocery story, gas station, and movie theater. The schools were perceived as strong and jobs were available, if not plentiful. Many city dwellers still did not lock their doors or windows. It was a user-friendly world. (Courtesy Decatur Public Library.)

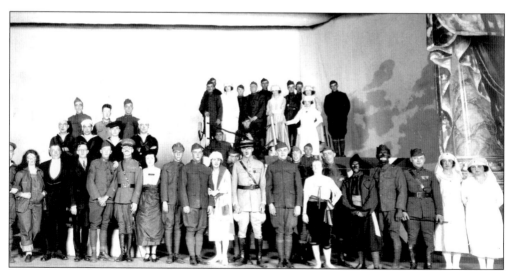

CAST PHOTO. On May 11 and 12, 1921, a local group of thespians performed *Heaven, Hell, or Hoboken*, a play based on the very recent World War I. Note the profusion of military uniforms from many different nations. Two actors appear in black face, which was common throughout the decade in stage and film productions, like Al Jolson's *The Jazz Singer* of 1927. (Courtesy of Decatur Public Library.)

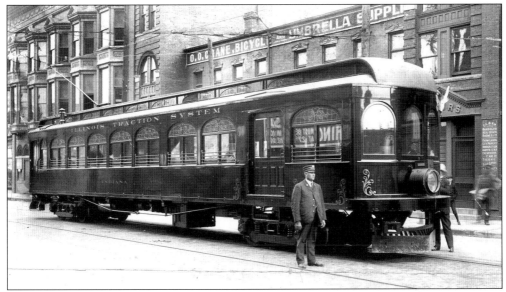

ILLINOIS TRACTION SYSTEM CAFÉ CAR. The Illinois Traction System, or the Interurban as it was popularly called, operated safe, clean commuter trains between a number of points in central Illinois and St. Louis for about half a century. It was not uncommon for the Interurban to stop in the middle of a cornfield to pick up a rural fare. Photo taken about 1920 on the 100 block of North Main Street. (Courtesy Decatur Public Library.)

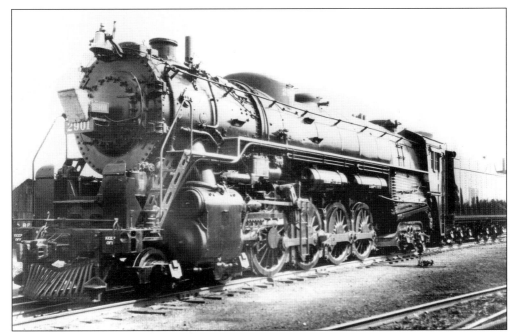

WABASH LOCOMOTIVE. This Wabash Railroad locomotive was photographed in Decatur in the 1920s. The twenties and thirties were golden decades for the railroads, and some of the most famous American trains were built during that period. By the 1940s, however, turnpikes and toll roads were giving trucks and buses a competitive edge, a process that peaked during the mid-1950s with the creation of the Eisenhower national expressway system. (Courtesy Decatur Public Library.)

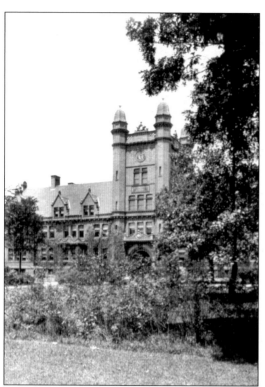

CLOCK TOWER, LIBERAL ARTS HALL. This frontal view of the Millikin campus, taken about 1929, shows the vegetation that had grown up since the building opened its doors in 1907. The twenties and thirties were difficult times at Millikin because of internal debates about governance and an ambiguous relationship with the Presbyterian Church. In the end, Millikin University became officially non-denominational, with only nominal ties to the church. And daily chapel attendance was ultimately abolished. (Courtesy Decatur Public Library.)

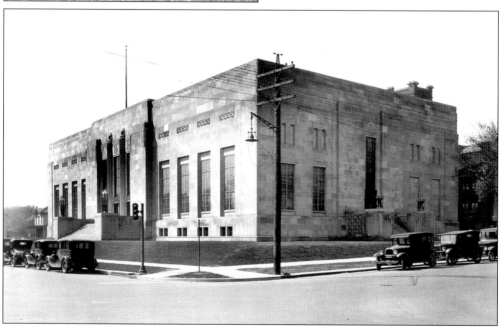

MASONIC TEMPLE. The cornerstone for this neoclassical masterpiece was laid March 24, 1928, and the building officially opened in January 1929. This photograph was taken a few months later. A.E. Staley was one of the principal benefactors of this building project, which coincided with the creation of the Staley Headquarters building, both in a similar style. (Courtesy Decatur Public Library.)

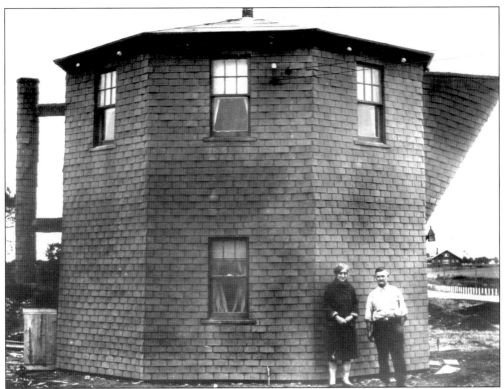

THE COFFEE POT. This east side eatery was at the height of its popularity when this photo was shot in 1929. Zany stunts and strangely-shaped buildings were typical of the decade. The trend was most noticeable later along the famous Route 66 from Chicago to Los Angeles, where restaurants were built in the shape of hamburgers, wigwams, and other whimsical forms. (Courtesy Decatur Public Library.)

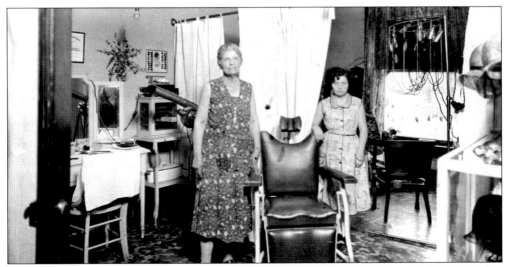

BEAUTY PARLOR. These beauticians are standing in an unidentified Decatur beauty parlor, with its formidable hair-curling and hair-drying implements. Note the naked light bulb hanging from the ceiling and the hats for sale at the extreme right. (Courtesy Decatur Public Library.)

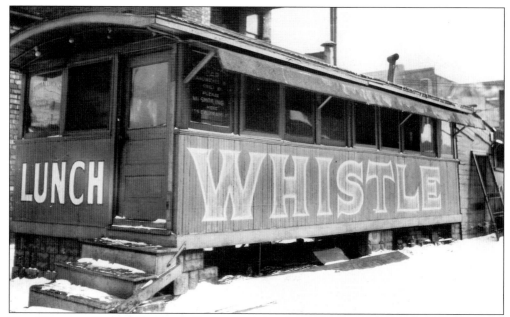

THE WHISTLE DINER. George Calfas, part of the Greek community that was active in the selling of ice cream, owned this diner that was fashioned from an old railway car. Business appears to be slow on the cold winter day when the photo was taken on February 25, 1928. The Whistle was the fast-food restaurant of its day. (Courtesy Decatur Public Library.)

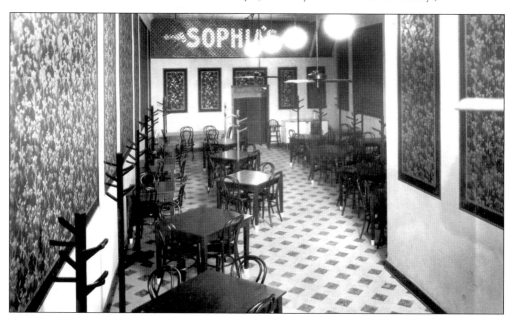

SOPHIA'S CHILLI PARLOR. Sophia's "Chilli" Parlor, as it was spelled in those days, was a spotless little venue in downtown Decatur, at 152 East Main, that was popular with business employees, shoppers, and the college set. Chili was big business in Central Illinois. Neighboring Springfield had many chili restaurants and canneries; at least one cannery is still in operation. Chili cook-offs are still popular in Central Illinois, and no county fair is complete without at least one stand selling chili dogs. (Courtesy Decatur Public Library.)

TRANSFER HOUSE, 1929. Four years before this photo was taken, a taxi cab rammed the side of the old Transfer House, nearly causing it to collapse and doing about $125 worth of damage—a lot of money in those days. Note the ladders leading to the flagpole atop the cupola. The water tower in the background has fortunately disappeared from sight. The camera is pointed northeast, with Merchant Street in the background. (Courtesy Decatur Public Library.)

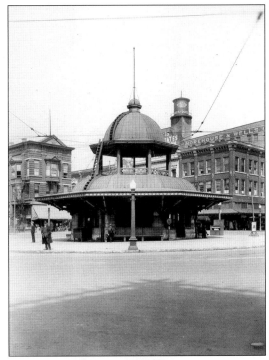

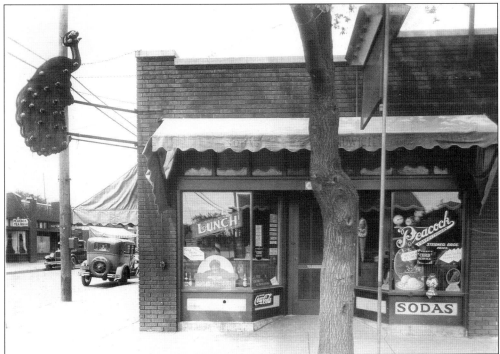

THE PEACOCK. This popular confectionery, located at 1202 East Wood Street, offered ice cream, sodas, hot barbecue, and curb service. Across the street was the Peacock Tea Room. A metal peacock, with colored bulbs embedded in its "wings," attracted customers during the evening hours of operation. Photo taken in 1929. (Courtesy Decatur Public Library.)

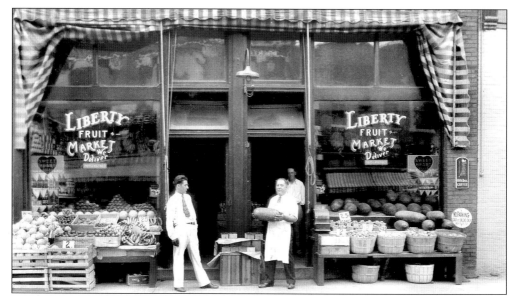

LIBERTY FRUIT MARKET. The Italian-American community dominated the fruit and vegetable business in Decatur during the twenties and thirties, among them Mike Lucuoco (pictured with the watermelon) and Ben Calamello (leaning against the awning support). Their store was located downtown at 141 East Prairie. As part of the user-friendly environment customers could expect fresh produce delivered to their doors. The photo was taken in the summer of 1929. (Courtesy Decatur Public Library.)

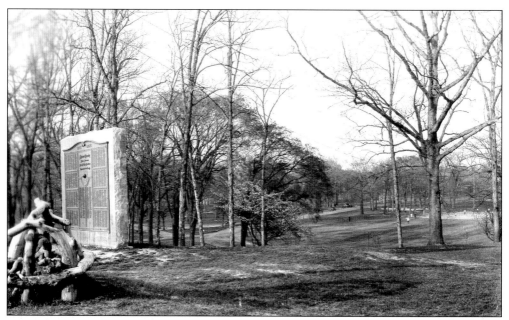

CIVIL WAR MEMORIAL TABLET. Erected during 1927 and 1928 at a cost of $3,500, this Civil War Memorial tablet in bronze and marble lists the names of 2,058 soldiers from Decatur and Macon County who fell in the Civil War. The memorial stands in Fairview Park and was dedicated on Flag Day in 1928. Decatur still has a Civil War Roundtable, which meets regularly. (Courtesy Decatur Public Library.)

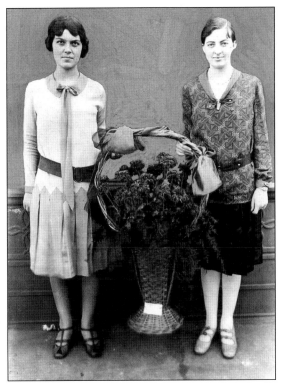

A Basket of Flowers. With bobbed hair, short skirts, and low-slung belts, Mrs. Naomi Moore (left) and Miss Arvilla Merritt (right) hold a big basket of flowers donated to them and their co-workers by Linn and Scruggs Department Store, October 5, 1928. They are standing on a downtown sidewalk. (Courtesy Decatur Public Library.)

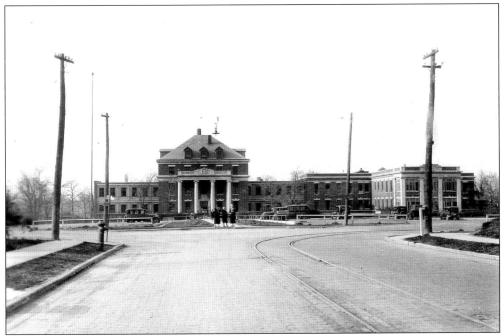

Decatur and Macon County Hospital. These buildings, shown in a 1929 photograph, date back to 1912 and form the nucleus of what today is called Decatur Memorial Hospital. The hospital is an institution presently seeing satellite clinics and other medical offices springing up all around it, creating a large "medical campus." (Courtesy Decatur Public Library.)

83

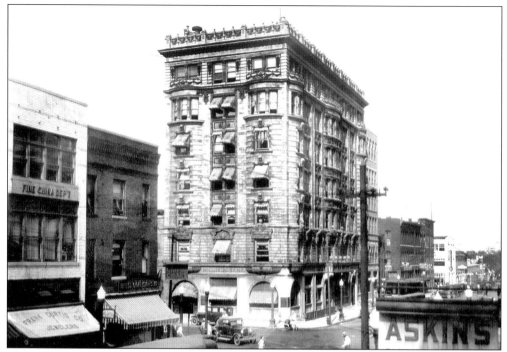

MILLIKIN BANK BUILDING, 1929. The Millikin National Bank was about 35 years old when this photo was snapped in 1929 as a young lady was running across East Main, apparently oblivious to the automobile bearing down on her. The venerable bank seemed totally integrated into this urban scene, but by 1979 it would have completely vanished from sight. (Courtesy Decatur Public Library.)

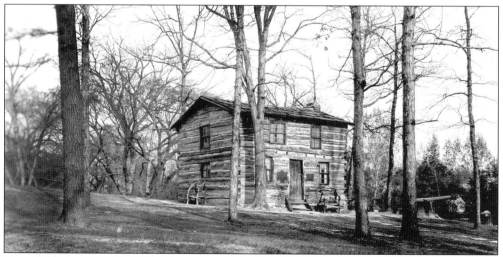

LOG COURTHOUSE, 1929. After it was replaced by a new brick building in 1839, this old log structure was moved west of Decatur where it was pressed into service as a barn. It then came into the possession of J.M. Clokey, who presented it to the Old Settlers Association about 1894, after which it was moved to several locations in the present Fairview Park. The barn has become one of the most recognizable and symbolic landmarks of Decatur and is now under the care of the Macon County Historical Society. (Courtesy Decatur Public Library.)

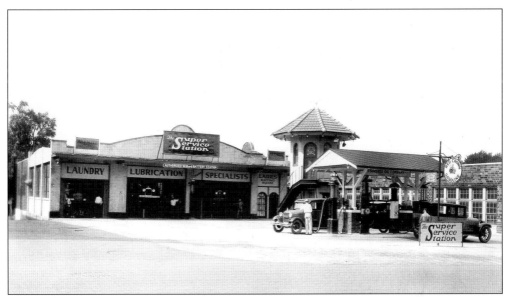

SUPER SERVICE STATION. Corwin Johns was manager of this station at Wood and Church Streets. Note the brick paving, the elaborate architecture, the Ladies Waiting Room (to the left of the tower), and the automobile "Laundry" on the far left of the building. America's love affair with the automobile was well under way when these premises were photographed in 1929. (Courtesy Decatur Public Library.)

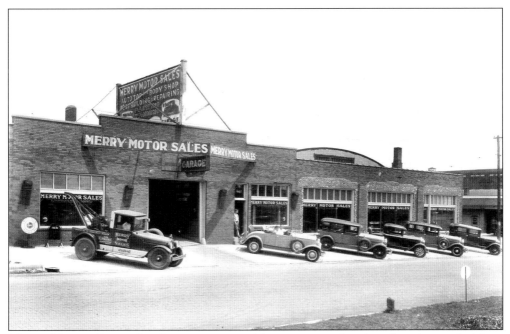

MERRY MOTOR SALES. Roadsters, coupes, and limousines are lined up for sale outside Merry Motors at 420 East Prairie Street. The year is 1929, and in a few short months very few people would be able to afford these beautiful new cars. Interestingly, Detroit continued to make—and sell—cars during the entire Depression, and it led the way to economic recovery with its many military contracts during the war years of 1941–1945.

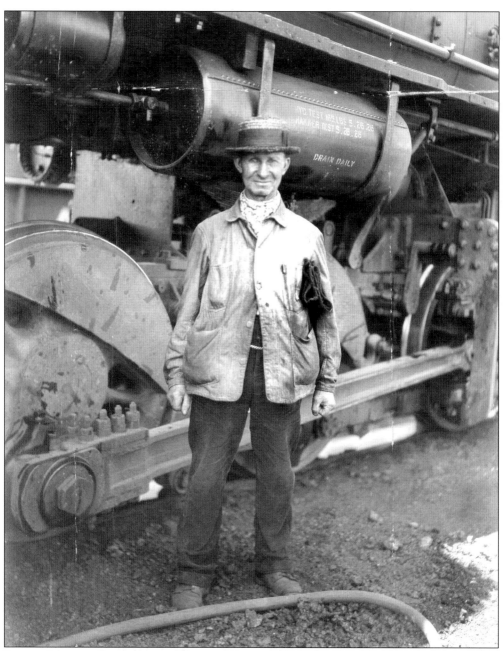

Joseph Swantz, Roundhouse Worker. For more than 50 years, from 1876 to 1927 or from the year James Millikin built his homestead on West Main and Pine to the year when Charles Lindbergh made his solo flight across the Atlantic, Joseph Swantz worked for the Wabash Railroad at the Decatur roundhouse facility. Fists clenched, he stands proudly in spite of his grimy clothes. Note the gold watch chain visible in the gap of his jacket. Swantz was born in 1849 and lived until he was 84, dying in 1933. Very few photographs exist of the individual carpenters, electricians, riveters, steel-makers, railroad engineers, machinists, and pipe-fitters who built and maintained the Decatur industrial culture. Joseph Swantz may thus be taken as a symbol for all those other proud and dedicated workers. (Courtesy Decatur Public Library.)

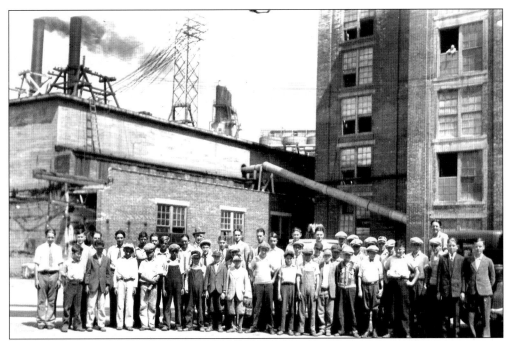

NEWSPAPER CARRIERS. On June 26, 1927, these young men, all newspaper delivery boys for the old *Decatur Review* posed in front of the operational buildings at Staley's Manufacturing Plant. Judging from the number of carriers, there was good newspaper circulation at this time, with radio just coming on the air and television still down the road. (Courtesy Decatur Public Library.)

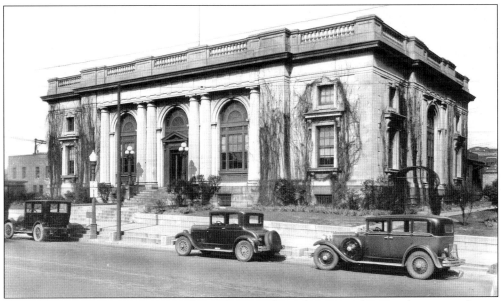

DECATUR POST OFFICE, 1929. In this early 1929 photo the encroaching ivy has not yet begun to bud, but customers are parked at the curb in a variety of vehicles, coupes, and sedans, old and new. The building would be rendered obsolete six years later when the new post office opened on Franklin. This old structure was at the corner of Main and Eldorado. (Courtesy Decatur Public Library.)

DECATUR PUBLIC LIBRARY HANDBOOK. The cover of this little booklet, published in 1928, shows the façade of the old Carnegie Library, which was directly across the street from the old post office. At the time, Warren F. Hardy, vice president of the *Decatur Herald* and one of the distinguished journalists in the city's history, served as the president of the Library Board of Directors. (Courtesy Decatur Public Library.)

Decatur Public Library

Its Resources
and
How To Use It

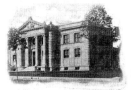

Main and Eldorado Streets

Library Hours . . . . 9 A. M. to 9 P. M.
Children's Room . . . 9 A. M. to 6 P. M.
SUNDAYS:
Reading and Reference Rooms . 2 to 5 P. M.

President of the Board of Directors:
WARREN F. HARDY
Librarian: MINNIE A. DILL

DECATUR · ILLINOIS
1928

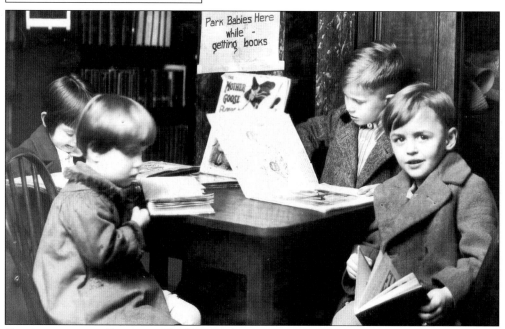

CHILDREN AT THE LIBRARY. The YWCA kindergarten students are sitting at a reading table in the children's corner of the old Carnegie Library. A copy of *Mother Goose* is on the table and the sign on the wall encourages parents to "Park Babies Here while getting books." The photo was taken in 1927. Children don't appear prominently in archival photographs until about a decade or so later. (Courtesy Decatur Public Library.)

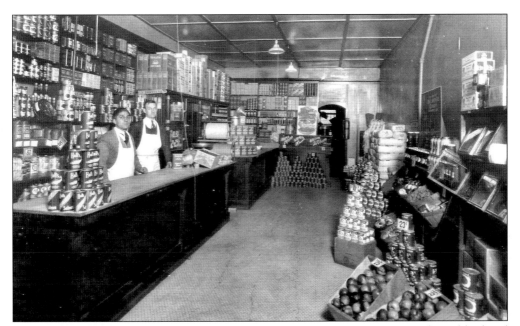

GROCERY STORE, 1920s. This unidentified photograph shows a fairly typical neighborhood grocery store of the period, before the "super" markets arrived on the scene. Customers generally presented the clerks with a list (oral or written), and the groceries were collected and boxed. Very few items were self-service. (Courtesy Decatur Public Library.)

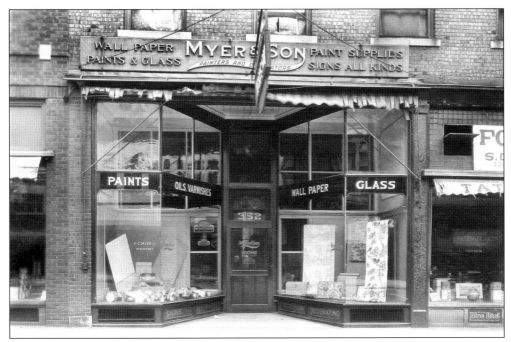

MYER AND SON. Martin Myer, one of the many industrious German immigrants, established this business in 1857. He moved twice before settling down at 250 North Park, then moved again to the location in this 1929 photograph, at 352 North Main. He sold paint, varnish, wallpaper, and glass, as well as offering decorator and sign painting services. (Courtesy Decatur Public Library.)

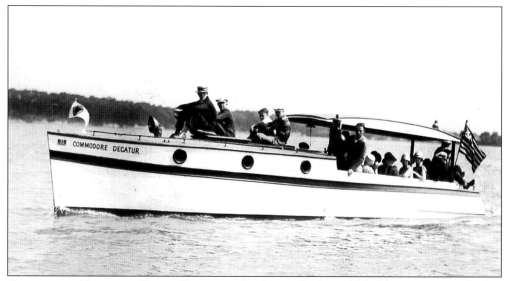

COMMODORE DECATUR CABIN CRUISER. This boat, which could hold up to 20 people, left Nelson Park every day at set times to provide five or ten mile cruises on Lake Decatur. On the five-mile trip, tickets cost 25¢ for adults and 15¢ for children. This profitable little venture was owned by Mr. C.R. Widdick of Decatur. (Courtesy Patrick Riley.)

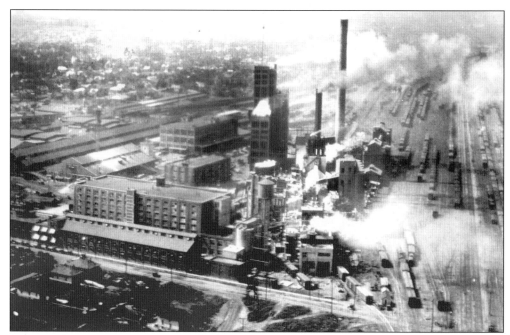

STALEY MANUFACTURING COMPANY, 1929. The Staley Company survived the imminent Great Depression, in spite of topsy-turvy markets, partly by emphasizing the newest product lines of crushed soybeans and soybean oil, both of which had many economical advantages. At this time, the company was unquestionably the flagship operation of the City of Decatur. In fact, the creation of Lake Decatur on June 28, 1922 and the damming of the Sangamon River had occurred earlier, so that the A.E. Staley Co. could finally slake its unquenchable thirst for water. (Courtesy Decatur Public Library.)

Three

MODERN TIMES
1930–1949

When Archer Daniels Midland moved to Decatur in 1939, the grain-processing giant was still a modest company building on the accomplishments of previous enterprises, much as General Motors had done in terms of automobile production in Michigan. ADM was empowered by the collective achievements of Shellabarger Mills, American Hominy, Ralston Purina, and the other grist mills operating in Decatur for over a century. The industry had come of age when A.E. Staley began buying out smaller mills in 1909; it then leapt forward again in 1922 when Staley began crushing soybeans. An entire infrastructure was already in place, awaiting a world-class operation like ADM, but 1939 was a somewhat dicey year to invest in Decatur. For although Decatur survived the Great Depression better than most mid-sized cities, the highly volatile commodities market affected everyone. Anxiety and opportunity existed side by side. Farmers in nearby Shelby and Moultrie Counties actually burned harvested ears of corn as fuel rather than dispose of them as trash. At the worst of times, no one would buy the grain, even at deflated prices. The Works Progress Administration did offer some government jobs in Decatur, chiefly in parkland improvement. The WPA also sponsored the murals in the 1935 Post Office Building—paintings executed in a kind of Thomas Hart Benton style, which are still visible today.

World War II kick-started the national economy, and the City of Decatur contributed valves and pumps (Mueller, Burks, Cash Valve) to the U.S. Navy and tank engines (Caterpillar/Victory Military Engines) to the Army. After the war, the Caterpillar engine plant became the Signal Depot, a giant military warehouse that was turned over to Firestone Tire in 1962. But Decatur's chief contribution was in personnel, men and women of all races, who served in all the branches of the military, leaving a rich photographic record of their accomplishments. When the war ended in August 1945, citizens of Soy City literally danced in the streets.

Returning soldiers began to sample the good life as previously rationed consumer goods, like appliances, automobiles, and tires, suddenly became available. New housing appeared, especially in the South Shores area. New families were pouring into the city, attracted by good-paying jobs and an expanding economy. The Fabulous Fifties were about to commence.

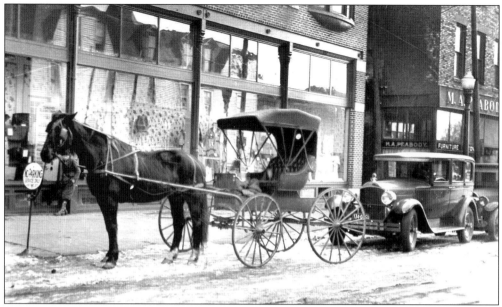

NO PARKING. The horse stands on the snow-dusted curb of East North Street in about 1930, oblivious to the "No Parking" sign in front and the cars behind. The storefront on the right belongs to Merton A. Peabody, who sold furniture, rugs, and stoves. He was in business for over three decades, from 1906 to 1940. (Courtesy Decatur Public Library.)

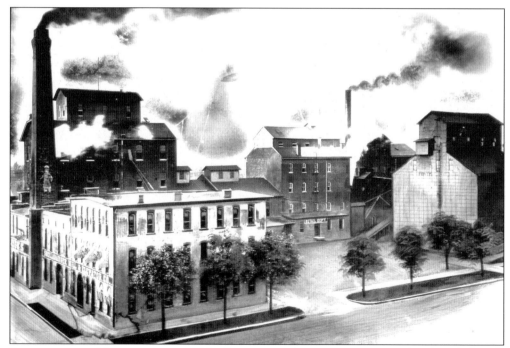

SHELLABARGER MILLS, ABOUT 1930. Decatur at this time was certainly identified with smokestack industries, which included the roasting and toasting of various grain products. David Shellabarger and his family owned and sold grain operations in Decatur for over 100 years, besides owning grain processing mills in Kansas. (Courtesy Decatur Public Library.)

Shellabarger Soyflake Flour. In this unidentified photograph, workers empty soy-based flour into one-hundred-pound sacks at the Shellabarger Grain Products Company. Such work was hot, physically draining, and potentially dangerous because grain dust is a highly flammable and explosive medium that can be set off, like a gas explosion, by the tiniest ignition. (Courtesy Decatur Public Library.)

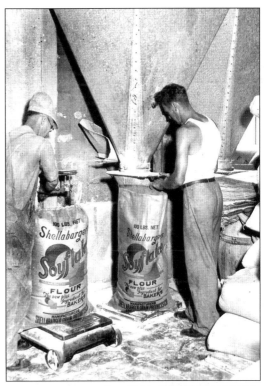

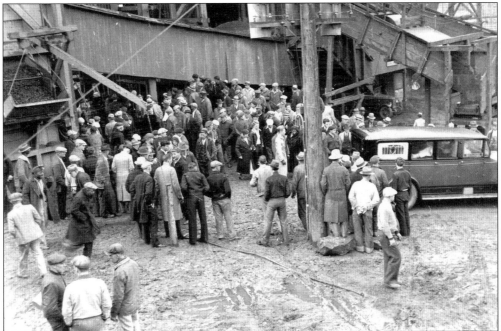

Coal Mine Accident. In November 1934, a serious accident at the Macon County Coal Company injured 10 workers. African-American and Caucasian miners watch as their unfortunate brothers are loaded into the waiting ambulance. A tough year economically, all of these men were lucky to have steady, good-paying employment. (Courtesy Decatur Public Library.)

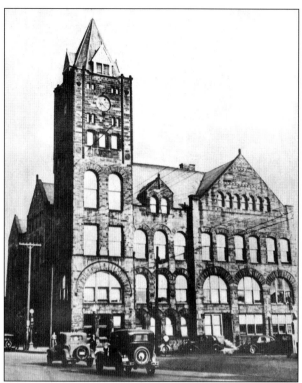

MACON COUNTY COURTHOUSE.
This building, which was actually
the third county courthouse,
stood at Wood and Water Streets
from 1891 to 1940, until the
present county building was
constructed to provide much-
needed additional space. This
photo is from the early 1930s.
(Courtesy Decatur
Public Library.)

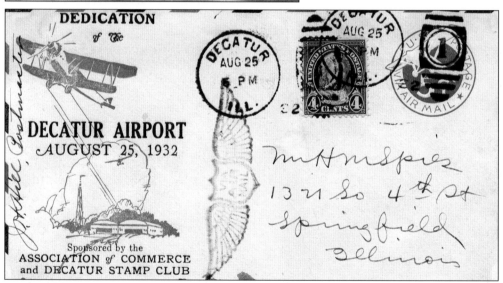

COMMEMORATIVE AIRMAIL ENVELOPE. This commemorative envelope, mailed to H.M. Spies
in Springfield, was issued by the Association of Commerce and the Decatur Stamp Club to
mark the dedication of the Decatur Airport on August 25, 1932. The airport is one more piece
of evidence that the city survived and actually expanded during the Great Depression, in this
instance adding an aerial "crossroad." Although aviation consultants predicted a great increase
in traffic in the 1960s and beyond, that potential was never realized because of the unforeseen
economic downturn. The Decatur Airport remains crucial to the future because it provides a
portal to the international marketplace. (Courtesy Decatur Public Library.)

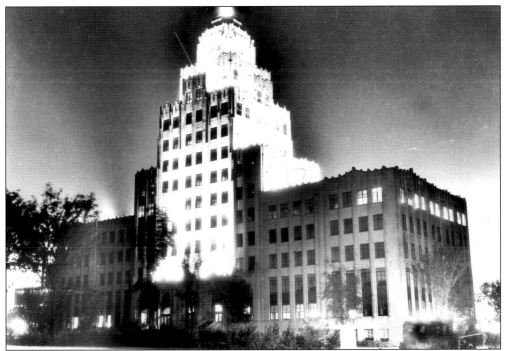

A.E. STALEY HEADQUARTERS BUILDING. This 1932 photo was taken about three years after this Decatur landmark was erected, at the very start of the Great Depression. In the evenings, colored lights would play upon the Art Deco façade, making it a visual delight that could be observed for miles around. (Courtesy Decatur Public Library.)

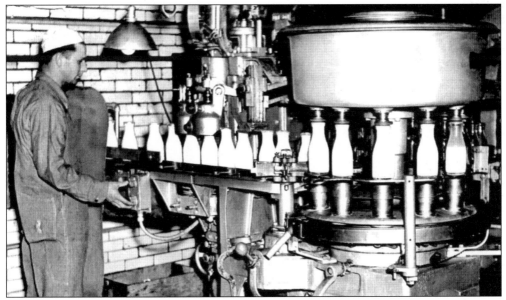

UNION DAIRY. A worker electrically fills milk quarts at the Union Dairy, at 304 South Main Street, in a photograph taken March 5, 1933. The milk business was clearly good, in spite of the fact that one out of every three wage earners was unemployed at the time. (Courtesy Decatur Public Library.)

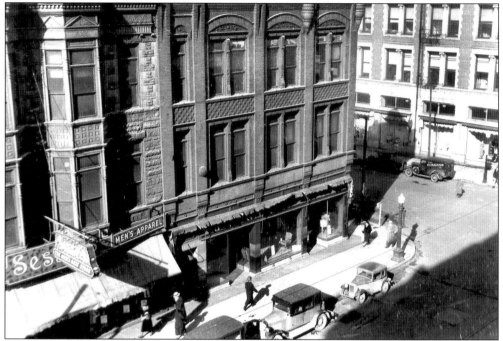

SESSELL'S MEN'S APPAREL. This photo of one of Decatur's classic men's stores was shot on February 2, 1934. The weather may have been cold and the times hard, but those conditions did not deter the shoppers from venturing out on this sunny, but wintry day. (Courtesy Decatur Public Library.)

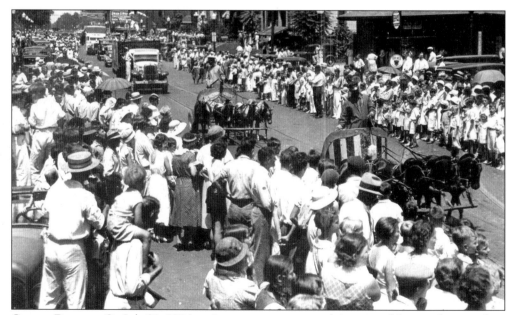

CIRCUS PARADE. On July 21, 1934, a circus came to town and, in spite of the very hot weather, crowds gathered along the 400 block of North Main to see the show. Just three decades earlier such a display of family informality—and light summer clothing—would have been unthinkable. (Courtesy Decatur Public Library.)

Wabash Freight Station.
Railroad work had not changed significantly in the previous two generations. This view of the Wabash water tower and freight station was taken on November 30, 1936. Business may have slowed down, but the railroads were still running, and keeping them running meant jobs for these Wabash employees. (Courtesy Decatur Public Library.)

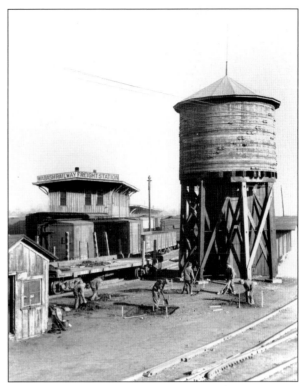

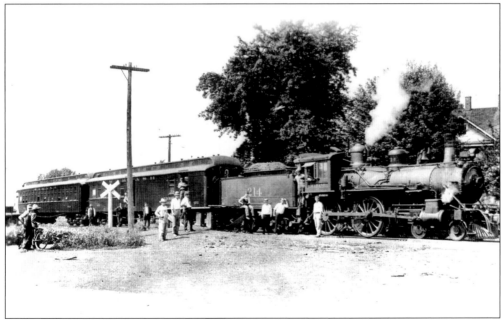

Wabash Steam Engine No. 214. Wabash Railroad Steam Engine No. 214 is shown here stopped in Hammond, Illinois, outside Decatur, on its final run, March 3, 1934. This photograph captures one of those soon-to-be-forgotten moments which somehow become special and interesting because they were saved from oblivion by the camera lens. Note the cyclist at the far left, and the man leaning on the coal car. (Courtesy Decatur Public Library.)

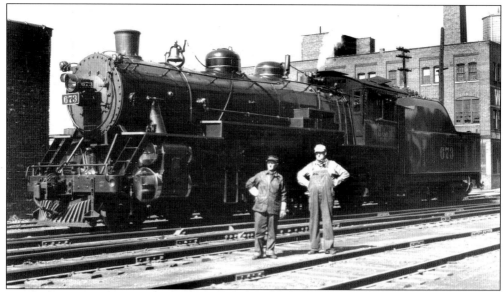

THE "BANNER BLUE." One of the most famous and beloved of the Wabash Railroad locomotives, Engine No. 673—the "Banner Blue"—was a transitional design somewhere between the classic locomotives and the newer, streamlined trains already appearing on the scene when this photo was taken, in about 1938 or 1939. Railroad workers experienced the same warm feelings for "their" trains as old-time sailors felt for their ships. (Courtesy Decatur Public Library.)

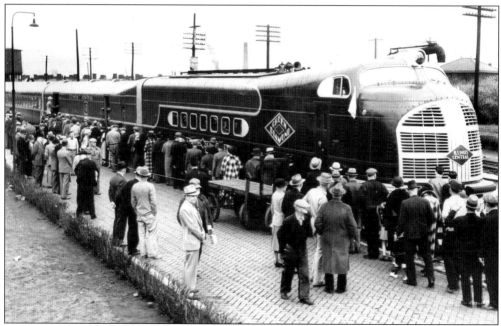

THE "GREEN DIAMOND." The "Green Diamond" was one of the most famous trains of the era, a sleek, diesel-powered locomotive belonging to the Illinois Central Railroad. Passengers are waiting to board on May 5, 1936. This same railroad once hired a Springfield lawyer named Abraham Lincoln to handle a big piece of litigation, which netted him $5,000, although he had to sue the company to receive his fee! (Courtesy Decatur Public Library.)

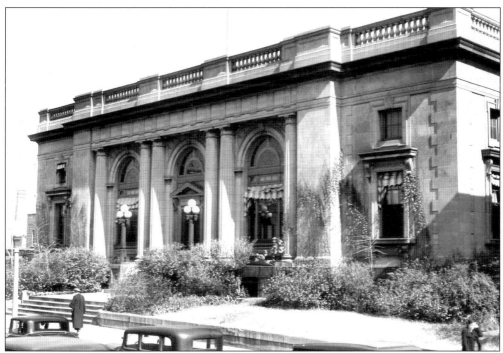

OLD POST OFFICE BUILDING IN 1935. Shortly after this photo was taken on October 18, 1935, the new post office opened on Franklin Street. Note the ivy on the portals and the awnings above the high windows. This fine old building might well have served any number of purposes—an art museum, for example—if the philosophy of adaptive reuse had been popular in 1935. (Courtesy Decatur Public Library.)

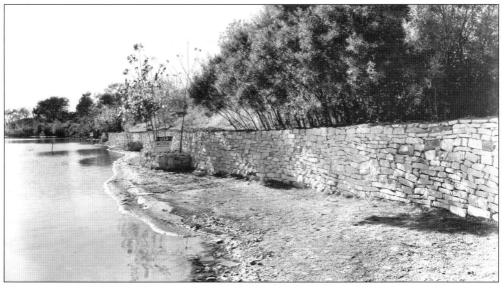

WORKS PROGRESS ADMINISTRATION WALL. Under the administration of Franklin Delano Roosevelt, the Works Progress Administration made improvements to city, state, and national parks all over the country, including this stone retaining wall near the shore of Lake Decatur. The photograph was made about 1937. (Courtesy Decatur Public Library.)

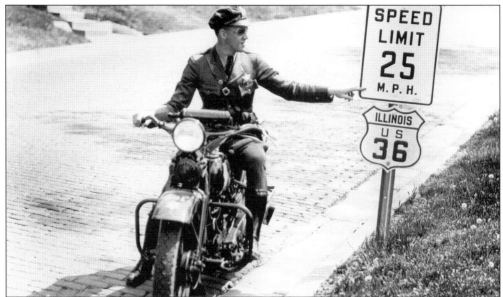

MOTORCYCLE POLICEMAN. The "long arm of the law" is literally pointing to the posted speed limit on brick-paved West Main Street, then known locally as "old Route 36" before Eldorado Street, a few blocks north, became Route 36. The photograph was made on May 8, 1936. (Courtesy Decatur Public Library.)

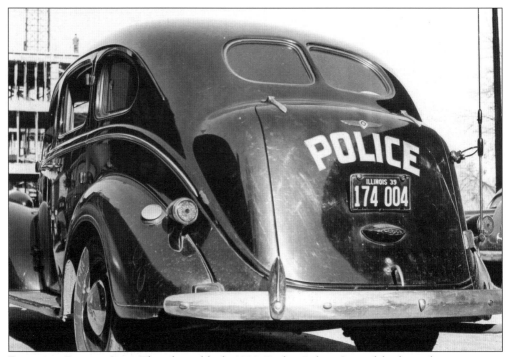

DECATUR POLICE CAR. This shiny black 1939 Dodge Police Special had just been put into service when the photograph was taken in 1939. The Decatur Police Department was rather well equipped during the thirties, in spite of the economic restraints and lower tax revenues. World War II started about a month after this photo was made. (Courtesy Decatur Public Library.)

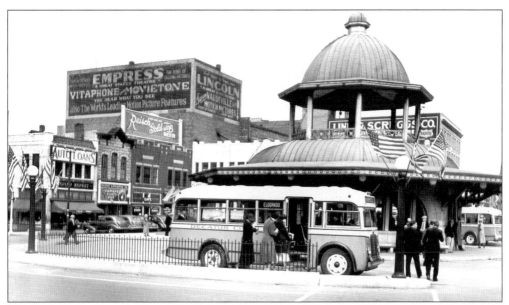

TRANSFER HOUSE, 1937. Taken November 13, 1937, this photograph of the old Transfer House shows new curbing and a wrought-iron fence, making the area serve as the central bus stop for the new Decatur city buses, which had just come into use during the 1936 fiscal year. The camera is pointed in a northerly direction. (Courtesy Decatur Public Library.)

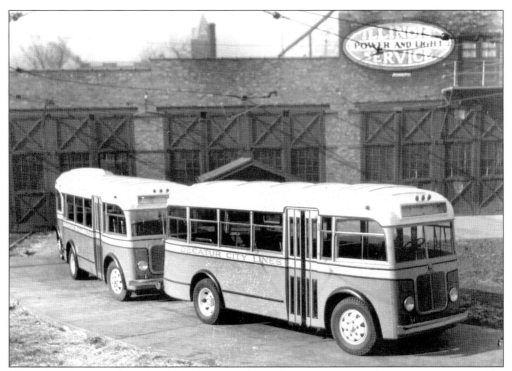

NEW CITY BUSES. These 1936 additions to the city's transportation fleet seem rather small by today's standards—they are about the size of a 16-passenger van. The buses are garaged on the premises of the Illinois Power and Light Service building. (Courtesy Decatur Public Library.)

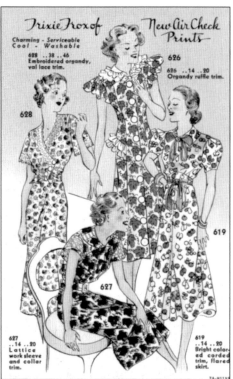

TRIXIE FROX. "Trixie Frox" were the latest thing in women's fashion, according to this postcard-advertisement from Osgood and Sons, one of the five major garment manufacturers operating in Decatur between 1880 and 1980. Postcard dates to the late 1930s. (Courtesy Patrick Riley.)

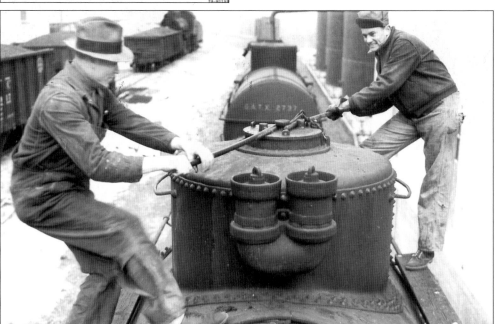

ADM WORKERS. This photograph was made on December 14, 1939, and Archer Daniels Midland had just come to Decatur, eventually acquiring property owned by such old-line mills as Shellabarger, Spencer-Kellogg, and Ralston Purina. The present global giant stood on the shoulders of these smaller companies. The two workers are shown loosening an aperture on a tank car. (Courtesy Decatur Public Library.)

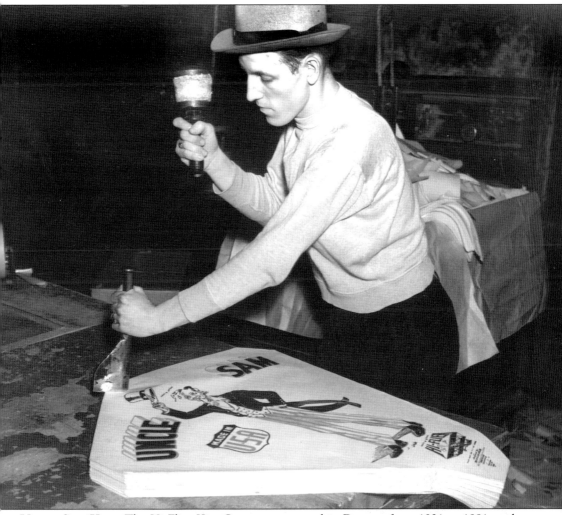

UNCLE SAM KITE. The Hi-Flier Kite Company operated in Decatur from 1921 to 1981, and the Uncle Sam kite was one of its all-time best sellers. In this March 24, 1938 photograph, a worker pounds a mechanical stapler with a mallet, finishing the crown of the kite. At a time when bread-lines and soup kitchens were still common sights in big cities, Decatur could offer jobs to people making kites, a small measure of the basic economic stability and diversity of the city. (Courtesy Decatur Public Library.)

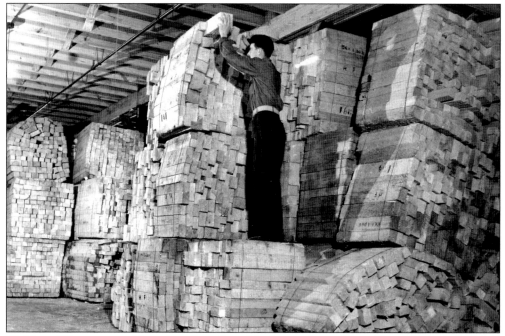

HI-FLIER WAREHOUSE. These bundles of wood had been shipped from Ecuador, specifically for use in the Hi-Flier Kite. The Hi-Flier employee stands on one stack of wood to reach above his head in a quest for the appropriate beam to be quickly reduced to kite-making specifications. (Courtesy Decatur Public Library.)

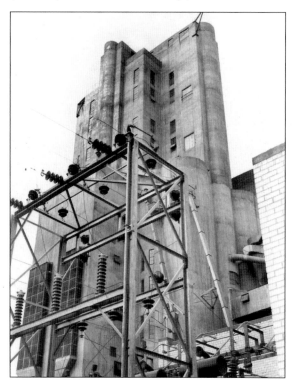

ADM ELEVATOR. This view of the ADM elevators and power sub-station was made on December 14, 1939. Along with A.E. Staley, ADM led the way in discovering new applications for corn, soybeans, and the many byproducts of food science, including high-fructose corn syrup, glutens, and starches. Other products went into salad oil, baby food, cosmetics, paint, ink, ethanol fuel, and baked goods. (Courtesy Decatur Public Library.)

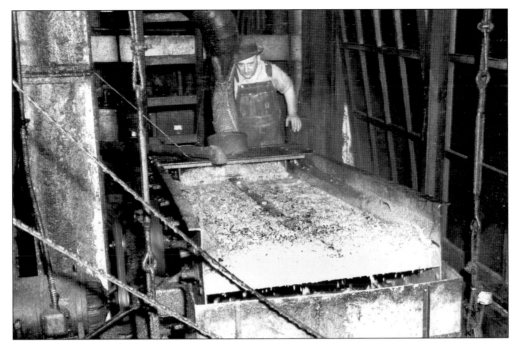

STARCH SEPARATOR. This photo was taken about 1940 and shows an A.E. Staley employee operating a starch-gluten separating machine. Raw corn and soybeans may have entered the gates of the plant, but the products that exited were varied and chemically sophisticated, "value-added" in today's economic parlance. (Courtesy Decatur Public Library.)

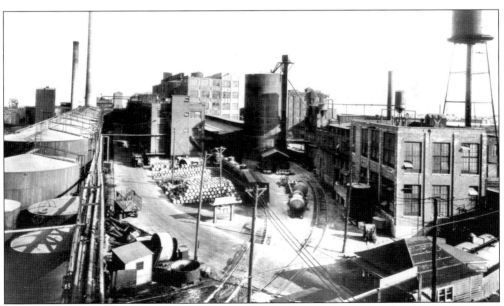

SPENCER-KELLOGG, 1939. This photograph of a typical grain-processing layout shows the rail lines, stacked barrels, vats, storage tanks, water towers, processing buildings, and smokestacks of Spencer-Kellogg, just prior to acquisition by ADM. Out of such apparent disarray came a dizzying assortment of products, including the humble corn flake and familiar household brands like Sta-Puf Fabric Softener and Staley Syrup. (Courtesy Decatur Public Library.)

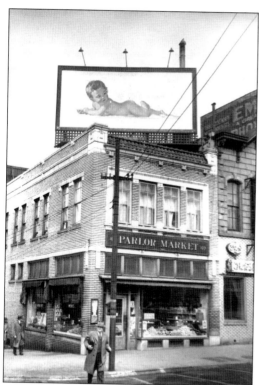

THE PARLOR MARKET. Made about 1940, this photograph shows the northwest block of Lincoln Square, and the Parlor Market at the corner of North Main and West Main—the same block that to the right contains the Hue Singleton Building. The Parlor Market site changed hands many times, but notably housed El Dora's Fashions in the 1980s. (Courtesy Decatur Public Library.)

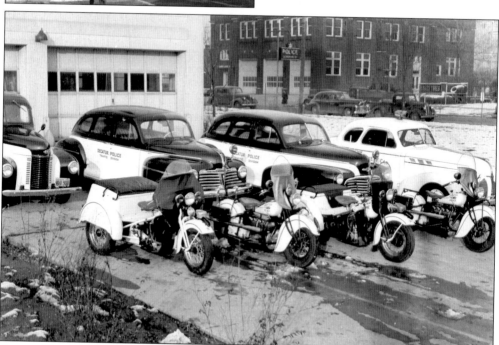

POLICE VEHICLES. These squad cars and three-wheeled motorcycles were on display at the Decatur Police Department Traffic Bureau on November 24, 1941, during the Thanksgiving holiday season. Two weeks later, the Imperial Japanese Government bombed Pearl Harbor, and the United States declared war on Japan. (Courtesy Decatur Public Library.)

WORLD WAR II AVIATOR. This photograph shows a smiling J.R. Aldenifer on May 24, 1941, just before the outbreak of the war. His geographical location, rank, and service affiliation are unknown. (Courtesy Decatur Public Library.)

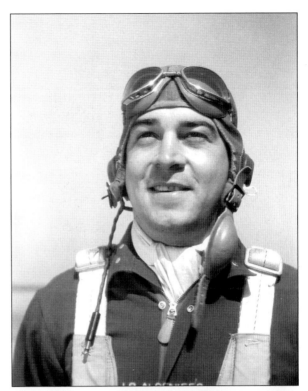

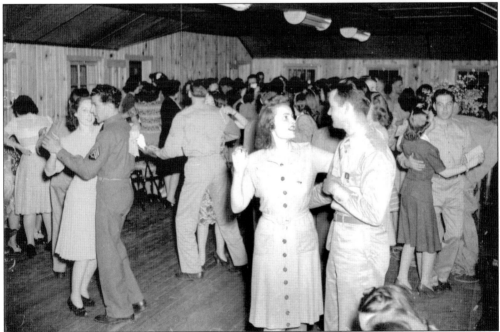

ENTERTAINING THE TROOPS. These local ladies are shown dancing with recent recruits at the U.S. Army Tent and Rest Camp at Lake Decatur on the evening of its dedication, May 24, 1942. As in the previous war, Decatur provided various amenities for troops coming through the city, including refreshments at the Union Depot. (Courtesy Decatur Public Library.)

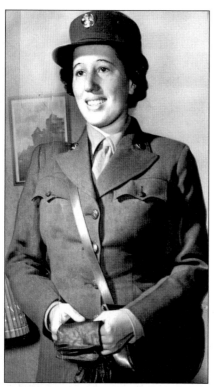

WILMA HAWKINS, WAC. Wilma P. Hawkins, daughter of Mr. and Mrs. D.C. Hawkins of Decatur, served as the first African-American WAC from Decatur. She was on a five-day furlough, recently arrived from a training stint in Iowa, when this photograph was snapped on November 8, 1942. (Courtesy Decatur Public Library.)

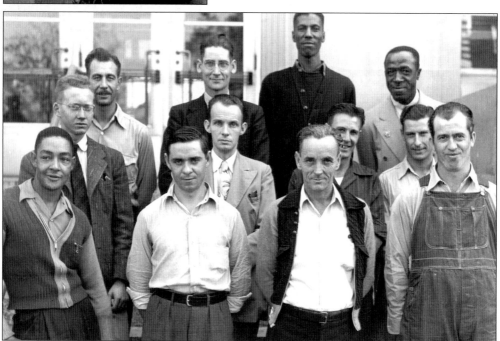

DECATUR DRAFTEES, 1942. This group photograph could stand as a cross-section of American society, since it shows a mixture of races and social classes in these 12 draftees, who were waiting to be bussed to Peoria for further testing and processing. The photograph was taken October 3, 1942. (Courtesy Decatur Public Library.)

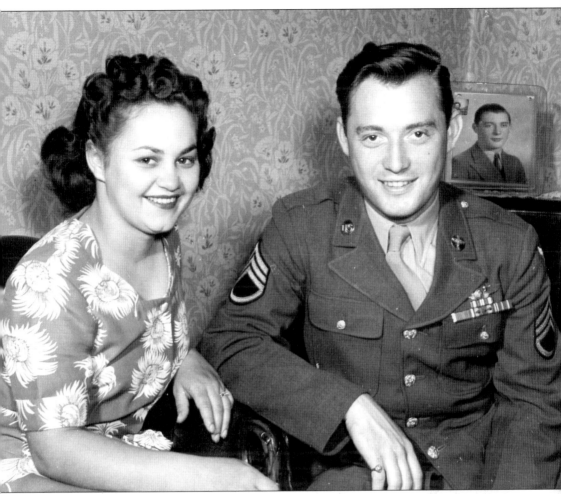

VELMA AND SAMUEL CONROY. Velma Hefner Conroy and Staff Sergeant Samuel E. Conroy were married only three weeks before this photograph was taken on June 4, 1944. The smiling couple was pictured in the home of his parents, Mr. and Mrs. J.H. Conroy, at 1185 West Forest Avenue. Sergeant Conroy had recently returned from an airfield in England, after having flown 25 missions over Germany as a waist gunner on a bomber. He was a decorated hero, having been awarded the Purple Heart, the Air Medal, and the Distinguished Flying Cross. Shortly after this photo was taken, he left for Miami and a new assignment. (Courtesy Decatur Public Library.)

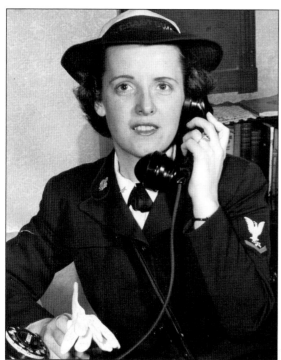

VIRGINIA CAUDILL. Virginia Caudill, daughter of Mrs. C.L. Hutson, volunteered for service in the Coast Guard. She left Palm Beach, Florida, where she had been training, to return home for Christmas in 1943, but she was involved in a train wreck in North Carolina. Miss Caudill suffered a minor back injury, but did arrive safely in Decatur the night before this photograph was taken on December 19, 1943. (Courtesy Decatur Public Library.)

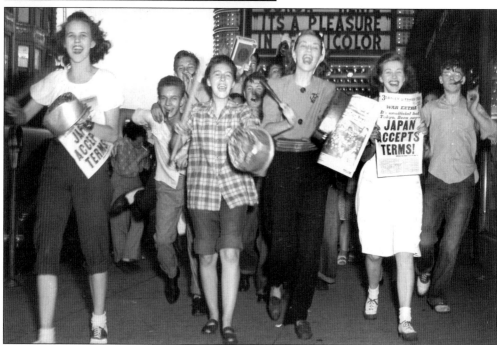

V-J DAY, 1945. This impromptu parade was composed of celebrating teenagers, some of whom are smoking cigars while others are beating on pots and pans to make noise. The "War Extra" edition of the paper sports the banner headline, "Japan Accepts Terms!" And the marquee of the Lincoln Theater in the background announces ice-skater Sonja Henie in *It's a Pleasure*. This photograph was taken August 14, 1945. (Courtesy Decatur Public Library.)

NAVAL FIREMAN DONALD MATHIAS.
Donald Mathias was home in nearby
Bethany, visiting his mother and
grandfather when this photograph was
made on May 20, 1945, about three
months before the end of the war. He
told the story of how his ship, the aircraft
carrier *Franklin*, was hit by Japanese dive
bombers while cruising in the Pacific. He
was trapped in a compartment for nearly
five hours with two dozen of his fellow
crewmen, and reported that even the
atheists "saw the light." (Courtesy
Decatur Public Library.)

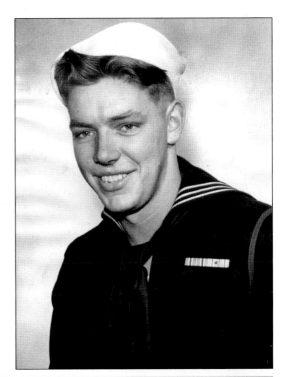

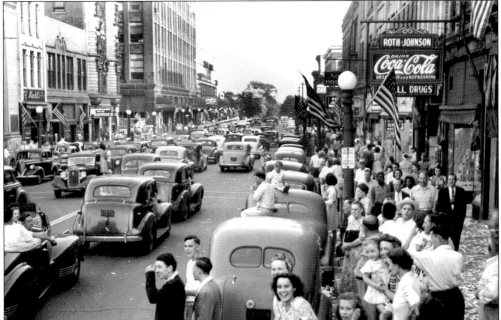

VICTORY CELEBRATION. Another photograph taken on V-J Day, August 14, 1945, shows the
heavy crowds and streams of traffic in downtown Decatur. The war had lasted four years for
Americans, six for Europeans, and the previous decade had seen a worldwide depression. It is
small wonder, then, that peacetime meant the unleashing of a pent-up demand for every
consumer good imaginable, as well as the desire to start new families. Thus, the Baby Boom was
born. (Courtesy Decatur Public Library.)

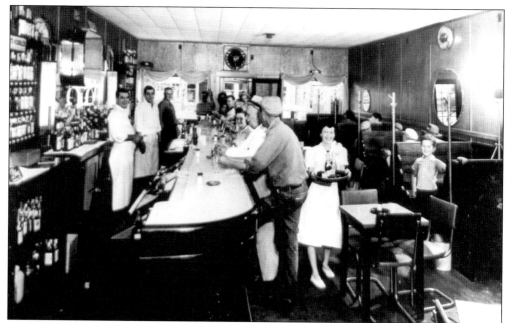

ESKER'S TAVERN. Esker's is the quintessential Decatur neighborhood tavern, a favorite during the World War II era and afterwards. It opened in 1941, occupying the site of a former grocery store and bar. Everyone seemed to be in a good mood when this photograph was taken in the late 1940s, including the bartenders, waitress, and the little patron on the right. (Courtesy Decatur Public Library.)

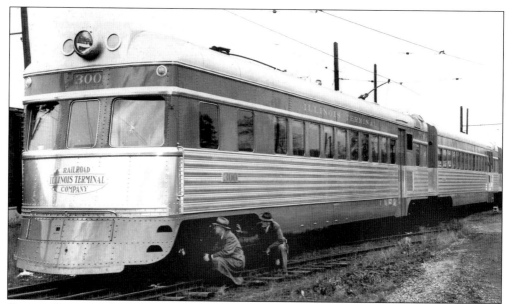

CITY OF DECATUR INTERURBAN TRAIN. This locally famous train helped to transport Decatur wives and mothers to do war work at the munitions plant in Illiopolis, a few miles westward. The artillery shells they produced undoubtedly killed many German and Japanese foes, helping to shorten the war. One could ride the Interurban to Danville in the northeast or St. Louis in the southwest—and most points in between. (Courtesy Decatur Public Library.)

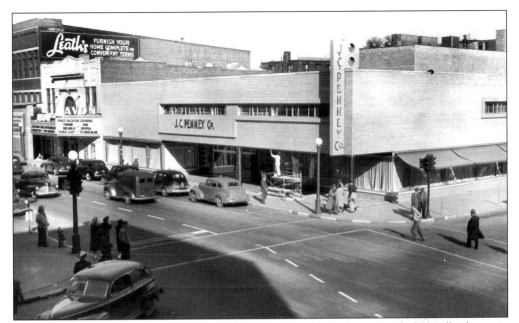

J.C. PENNEY CO. This corner, at North and Water Streets, has remained physically the same for nearly 60 years, even if the occupants of the buildings have naturally changed. The Avon Theater has been resurrected by manager Skip Huston, and it now shows first-run art and independent films, making Decatur one of the best venues in Illinois for such offerings outside Chicago. (Courtesy Decatur Public Library.)

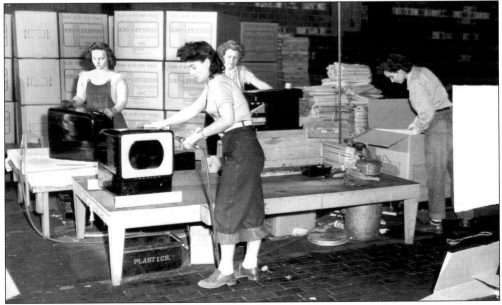

MAKING TELEVISION CABINETS AT GENERAL ELECTRIC. These women were employed by the General Electric Plastics Division, and they were making television cabinets to be used in Crosley Televisions. Note the informal attire, especially the cuffed "dungarees," pastel sweater, and contrasting belt of the lady in the foreground—the latest in shop floor chic for December 29, 1949. (Courtesy Decatur Public Library.)

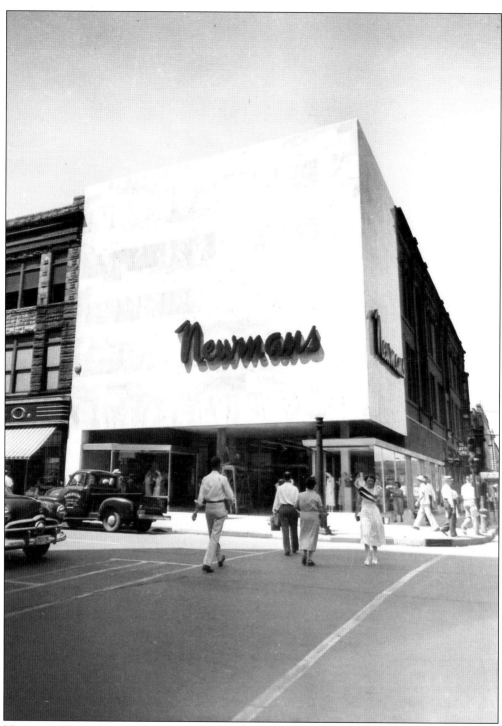

NEWMANS DEPARTMENT STORE, 1950. On this sunny day in August of 1950, the shoppers in downtown Decatur seem to be striding purposefully into the new decade, and the memories of wartime are slowly fading away. Note the postwar Ford sedan and Chevrolet pickup truck in the left center of the photograph. (Courtesy Decatur Public Library.)

Four
SOY CITY
1950–2004

The euphoria of the 1950s and early 1960s was enhanced by the arrival of new enterprises, like the General Electric Plant (1947–1975), the Firestone Tire Plant (1963–1989), and the mammoth Caterpillar Plant (1954), which offered generous wages, salaries, and benefits to its army of employees. Decatur had become an internationally competitive city, selling its processed grains, oils, and syrups (as well as pumps, valves, and road-graders) all over the globe. Then, in 1976, the city added another crossroad in the form of Interstate Highway 72.

Then came the dark days of the late 1970s, followed by the equally troubling 1980s and 1990s. The process began with alarming double-digit inflation and the symbolic loss of Decatur's title as Soybean Capital of the World. Strikes and labor turmoil typified the period, and the city lost population in general and many of its skilled laborers in particular. In one fateful week at the turn of the new century, Decatur led the nation in unemployment. Hickory Point Mall, which was located just beyond the city limits (near the new Interstate 72) in Forsyth, brought increasing tax revenue and exponential growth to that small town, while undercutting Decatur's tax base and luring away old downtown stores, like Sears, J.C. Penney, and Bachrach.

Yet Decatur rebounded. By the late 1970s the city was already becoming more ethnically diverse, a trend reflected in the many new Mexican and Chinese restaurants. Archer Daniels Midland became "supermarket to the world." And national fast-pitch baseball tournaments, national speedboat races on Lake Decatur, and the Decatur Celebration became eagerly anticipated annual events. Central Park and other venues downtown became the sites of art fairs, ethnic food fairs, and farmer's markets. In reaction to the loss of many cultural icons, serious preservation groups sprang up, like the Near West Restoration and Preservation Society and the Heritage Network. The Macon County Conservation District expanded bike and hiking trails. The Children's Museum of Illinois and the Hieronymus Mueller Museum both opened to the public. In 2004, as the city celebrated its 175th birthday, builders of the Wabash Crossing project were creating two square city blocks of new housing, and the city council was considering plans to preserve and highlight the city's treasures, including the most enduring symbol of Decatur history—the Transfer House.

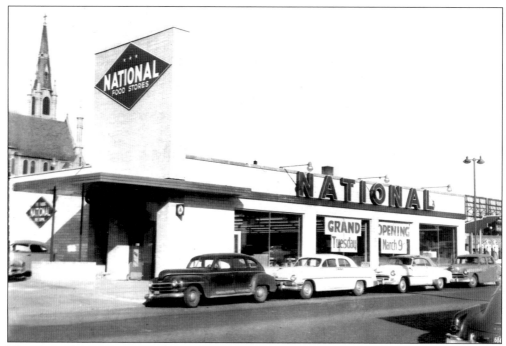

NATIONAL SUPERMARKET. The grand opening of this National Supermarket at North and Broadway, on Tuesday March 9, 1951, marks the beginning of the end for the era of mom and pop neighborhood grocery stores. Cars and supermarkets are fairly reliable gauges of cultural changes in the decade of the 1950s. (Courtesy Decatur Public Library.)

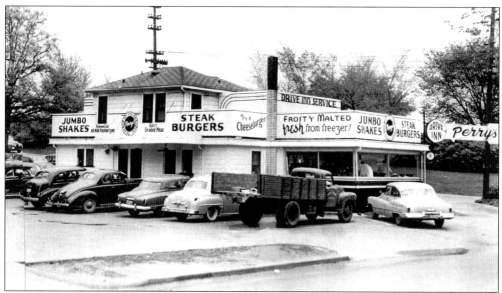

PERRY'S DRIVE INN. The 1950s drive-in restaurant combined cars, cheeseburgers, and jumbo shakes in a manner that proved irresistible to the average consumer. Perry's was a landmark on lower Twenty-second Street. The clientele must have been diverse on the day this photo was taken in about 1952, judging from the vintage and variety of the vehicles parked outside. (Courtesy Decatur Public Library.)

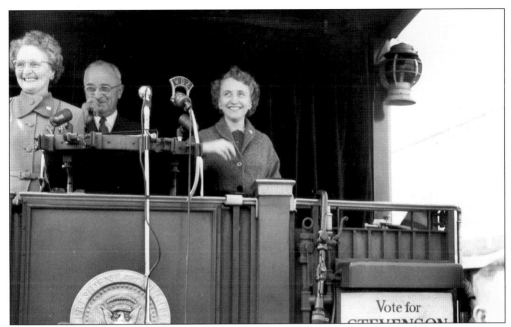

PRESIDENT HARRY S. TRUMAN. In 1952, President Truman, accompanied by his wife and daughter, made a "whistle stop" in Decatur to campaign on behalf of Adlai Stevenson, former governor of Illinois, who was a candidate for the presidency against Dwight David Eisenhower. Eisenhower, of course, won the election, but Stevenson later became ambassador to the United Nations under President John F. Kennedy. Note Decatur's radio station, WDZ, had its microphone strategically placed on the lectern. (Courtesy Decatur Public Library.)

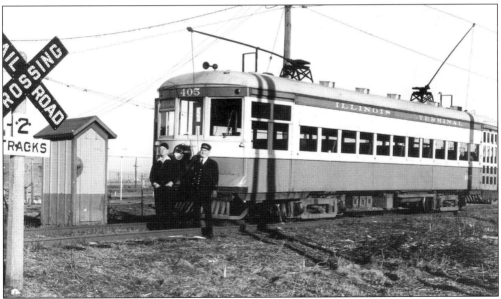

ILLINOIS TERMINAL RAILROAD. No. 405, known as the "Suburban Car," was one of the more popular trains on the Interurban System. This jovial conductor welcomed families, unattended children, elderly customers, and the occasional traveler with parcels or boxes to lug aboard. Unscheduled stops meant slow but personalized service for all the customers.

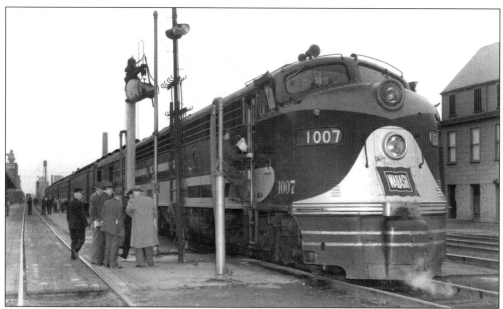

WABASH RAILROAD "BLUEBIRD." Probably the most beloved and remembered of all the Wabash trains to roll through Decatur, the "Bluebird" is about to depart from the station sometime in 1952. The Wabash "Cannonball," probably the most famous of all the Wabash trains, rolled through Decatur for the very last time on April 30, 1971. (Courtesy Decatur Public Library.)

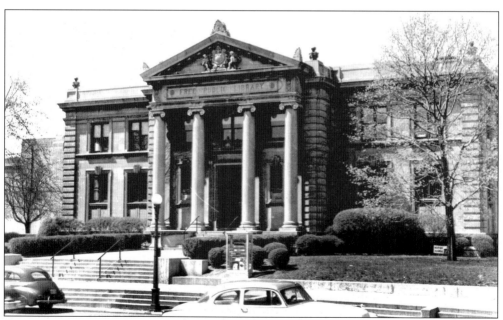

CARNEGIE PUBLIC LIBRARY. This building served the readers of Decatur from 1903 to 1971. It was demolished in October of 1972, in spite of the fact that it would have made a perfectly lovely art gallery, arts center, historical museum, small concert hall for string quartets or poetry readings, or venue for community meetings. The photograph was taken April 16, 1953. (Courtesy Decatur Public Library.)

POLAR ICE COMPANY. One of the many home-delivered products available in the Golden Era of small neighborhoods and personalized service was ice. Here, a worker is loading brown paper bags of Polar Ice onto a truck for delivery. The photo was taken on September 1, 1953, before the advent of polyethylene plastic bags. (Courtesy Decatur Public Library.)

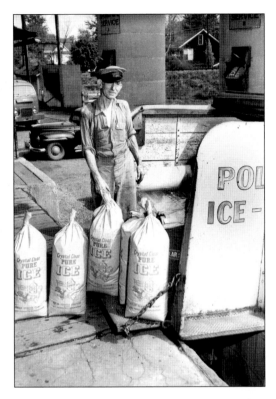

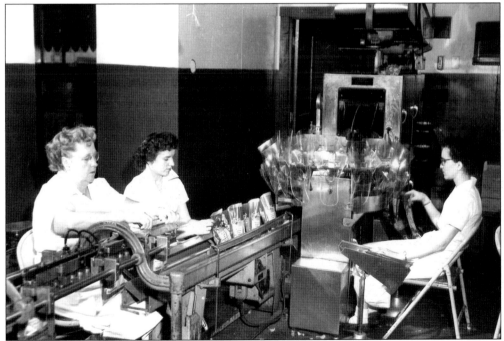

KELLY'S POTATO CHIP COMPANY. These women are involved in the process of sealing small bags of potato chips at the Kelly plant in 1954. Since 1921, at least one company has produced potato chips in Decatur, including Kelly, Crane, and Perfect brands. (Courtesy Decatur Public Library.)

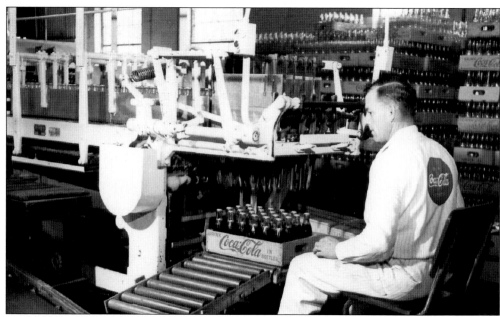

COCA-COLA BOTTLING COMPANY. In 1957, the Coca-Cola Bottling Plant was located on Franklin Street. The company then offered only one product—what is today called Classic Coke. Diet, lime, or vanilla versions were not available in that simpler world of the fifties. Here, the worker is inspecting the cased bottles as they roll off the bottling line. (Courtesy Decatur Public Library.)

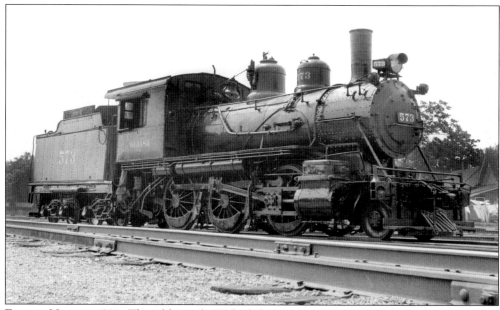

ENGINE NUMBER 573. This older-style Wabash locomotive was nearing the end of its service, as the newer, cleaner, and faster diesel-powered trains were becoming ever more numerous. The photograph was made on August 7, 1955, somewhere on the east side of Decatur. Note washing on the line in the extreme right, next to the cow-catcher of the locomotive. (Courtesy Decatur Public Library.)

HOME MILK DELIVERY. Although today's children may not believe it, there once was a time when milk and ice cream were delivered regularly to the front door of the home, even if all the "homemakers" may not have been as attractively turned out as this lady on May 11, 1958. (Courtesy Decatur Public Library.)

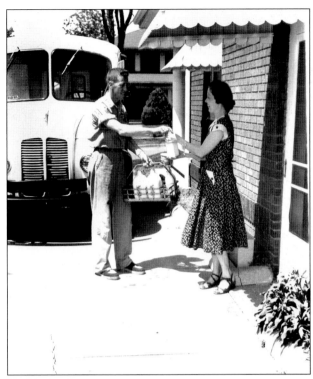

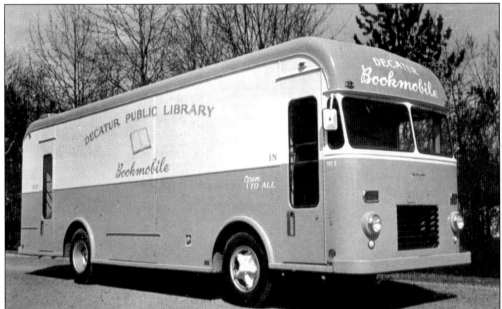

DECATUR BOOKMOBILE. This postcard image from the late 1950s shows one of the earlier Decatur Public Library Bookmobiles, a necessity even today because there is only one library and no outlying branches. For a small to mid-sized city, however, Decatur has always enjoyed outstanding library service. The library is an integral part of the community and its quality of life. Many organizational meetings and classes are held on the premises; book fairs and other cultural programs occur there regularly. (Courtesy Patrick Riley.)

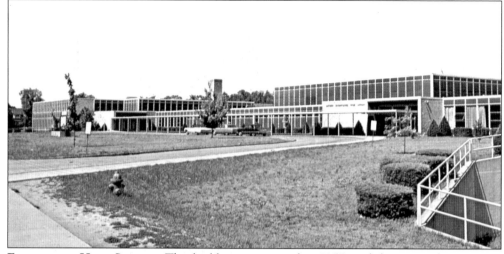

EISENHOWER HIGH SCHOOL. This building was erected in 1957, and the postcard image seen here dates to about 1960. Eisenhower was named after the popular president of the fifties, and the school was designed to serve the south side of the city, as MacArthur and Stephen Decatur served the west and north, respectively. Stephen Decatur is now a middle school, leaving the other two institutions as the only high schools in the city. (Courtesy Patrick Riley.)

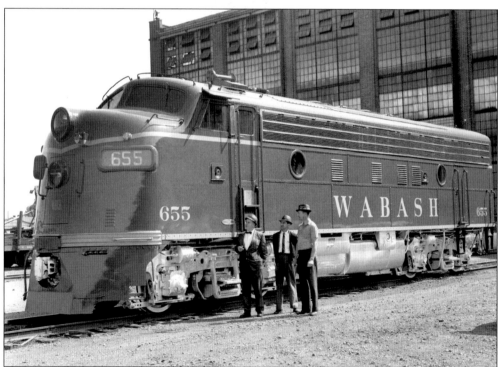

WABASH ENGINE NO. 655. On June 24, 1961, these Wabash employees are admiring the glossy coat of paint recently applied to Engine No. 655, a diesel-powered locomotive. As with all technological progress, this sleek new train nevertheless creates a certain nostalgic aura for the older, coal-burning engines, with their smokestacks, cowcatchers, and steam whistles. (Courtesy Decatur Public Library.)

SENATOR JOHN F. KENNEDY. As a senator campaigning for the presidency against Richard M. Nixon, John F. Kennedy visited Decatur in October 1959 and was photographed on the tarmac at the airport with State Senator Robert W. McCarthy, who used this photograph as a campaigning tool. (Courtesy Patrick Riley.)

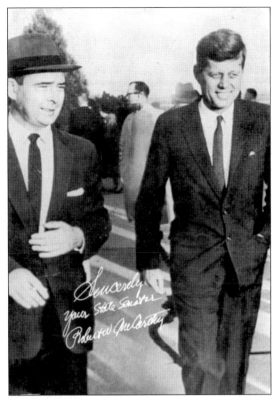

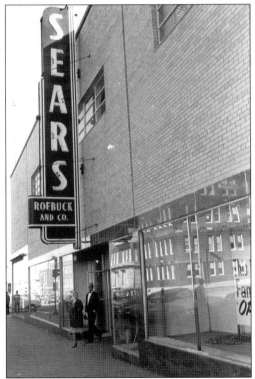

SEARS, ROEBUCK AND CO. In 1971, the old Carnegie Library was abandoned, primarily because of insufficient space to house the growing collections, and the Decatur Public Library moved to this building, which had been recently vacated by Sears. Then, in September 1999, the library followed in the footsteps of Sears again and moved to its present location on Franklin Street. Sears is now located in the Hickory Point Mall in Forsyth. (Courtesy Decatur Public Library.)

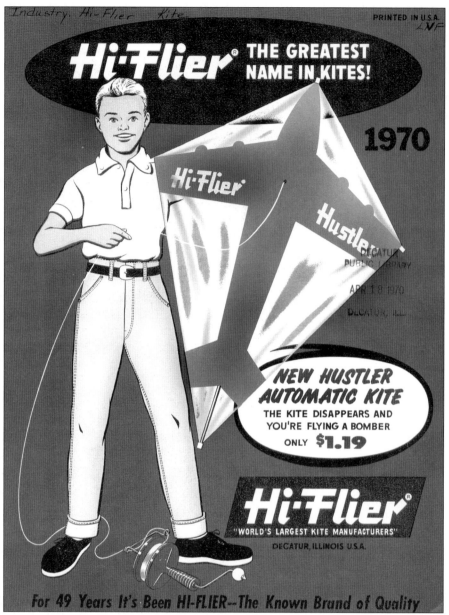

HI-FLIER HUSTLER KITE. This advertisement for the Hi-Flier Hustler kite dates to 1970, a rather turbulent time in the nation's history. The well-groomed young man in the picture seems blissfully unaware of the counter culture and the hippie style of fashion then prevalent. It is also worth noting that the Hi-Flier Kite Company billed itself as the "world's largest kite manufacturer." And it proudly listed Decatur, Illinois as its home base, a situation that would last only about one more decade, as Hi-Flier moved all its operations out of the city in 1981, one of the many losses that occurred during that dark decade and the following one. Although the payroll may not have been on a par with that of Staley Manufacturing or Archer Daniels Midland, Hi-Flier was a steady contributor to the economy of Decatur from 1921 to 1981. (Courtesy Decatur Public Library.)

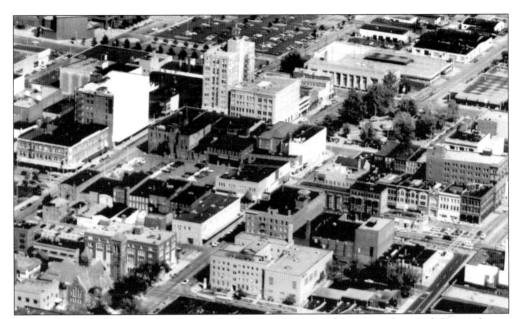

AERIAL VIEW OF DOWNTOWN DECATUR. This 1988 postcard is oriented toward the northeast. The new Civic Center can be seen in the upper left corner, and the tall white building in the top center is the Citizens National Bank. Lincoln Square is visible in the lower right side of the image. If one could see all the buildings that ever existed in the space of this photograph, there would be sufficient structures to fill several downtowns. (Courtesy Decatur Public Library.)

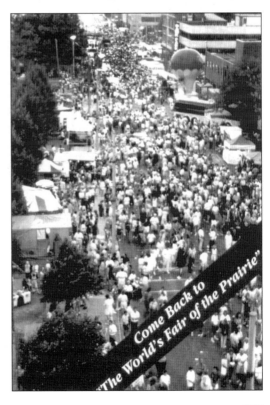

DECATUR CELEBRATION, ABOUT 1990. Part of what might be called the "Decatur Renaissance" is the highly successful Decatur Celebration, held annually during the first week of August, when the downtown area becomes a virtual amusement park with food vendors, rides, musical acts, and other attractions. Attendance has always been strong and tends to grow a little every year. In this postcard image, the celebration is billed as "The World's Fair of the Prairie." New signage at the entrance to the city limits, north on U.S. 51, and south on U.S. 36, proclaim Decatur as "The Pride of the Prairie." (Courtesy Patrick Riley.)

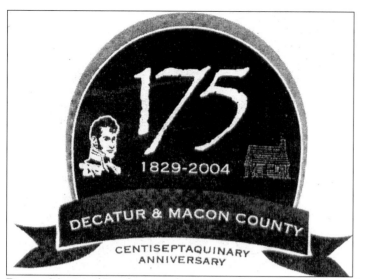

CENTISEPTAQUINARY ANNIVERSARY LOGO. On April 14, 2004, the Heritage Network, an association of over 25 local museums, county and city agencies, historical societies, and preservation groups, organized a 175th birthday party for the city and adopted this logo for the event. It pictures Commodore Stephen Decatur on the left, and the Lincoln Courthouse on the right. Appropriately, the Decatur Municipal Band was on the program. The event included a free lunch of ham and beans with apple cobbler. Local Historian Bob Sampson spoke on the history of the city and many residents appeared in period costumes. (Courtesy of the author.)

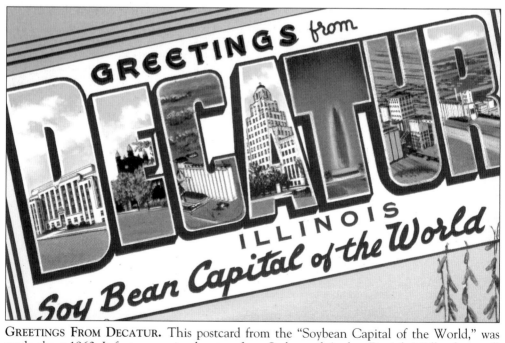

GREETINGS FROM DECATUR. This postcard from the "Soybean Capital of the World," was made about 1960. It features grain elevators from Staley and Archer Daniels Midland, as well as the Millikin University clock tower, the Staley Headquarters Building, and the Central Park Fountain. (Courtesy Patrick Riley.)

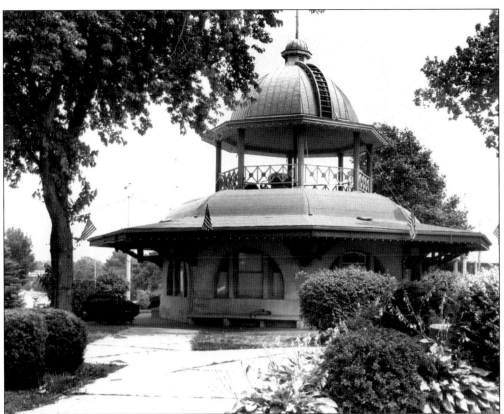

THE TRANSFER HOUSE, AUGUST 1996. This documentary photograph of the Transfer House in its present location in Central Park is the work of photographer Don Baker, who captured the old structure on a sunny afternoon when it was bedecked with American flags. Originally intended as a ticket booth and transfer point for riders of the streetcar system, this building slowly became the most recognizable landmark of Decatur. It has served as a kind of benchmark upon which the stream of historical images could somehow be measured and better understood. Everything around it seems to change, but the Transfer House endures. (Courtesy Dale Irwin, *The Century of Change.* Used with permission.)

FOR FURTHER READING

Anderson, Karen and Dayle Cochran Meredith. *Decatur Business: A Pictorial History*. St. Louis: G. Bradley Publishing, 1995.

Banton, O.T., ed. *History of Macon County*. Decatur: Macon County Historical Society, 1976.

Johns, Jane Martin. *Personal Recollections of Early Decatur, Abraham Lincoln, Richard Oglesby, and the Civil War*. Decatur: Daughters of the American Revolution, 1912.

Knoepfle, John. *Poems from the Sangamon*. Urbana: University of Illinois Press, 1985.

Kyle, Otto. *Abraham Lincoln in Decatur*. New York: Vantage Press, 1957.

Meyer, Charlotte, et al. *Places and People in Decatur: 1900–1929*. Decatur: The Zonta Club, 1976.

Sampson, Bob. "Army of the Night." *Illinois Times*. July 7, 1994: 4-5.

Smith, John W. *History of Macon County, Illinois, from its Organization to 1876*. Springfield: Rokker's Printing House, 1876.

Smith, Madeline Babcock. Introduction by Dan Guillory. *The Lemon Jelly Cake*. Urbana: University of Illinois Press, 1998.

White, Florence Scott, ed. *Rural Schools of Macon County*. Decatur: Macon County Historical Society, 1978.